The Poetry is in the Pity

By

MILDRED DAVIDSON

BARNES & NOBLE BOOKS · NEW YORK
(a division of Harper & Row Publishers, Inc.)

Published in the U.S.A. 1972 by
HARPER & ROW PUBLISHERS, INC.
BARNES & NOBLE IMPORT DIVISION

ISBN 06 4915875

© Mildred Davidson 1972

Printed in Great Britain

1981

THE POETRY IS IN THE PITY

Contents

Acknowledgements

Acknowledgements are due to the following copyright owners and publishers for permission to quote from copyright material:

George Allen & Unwin Ltd and The Macmillan Company, New York: *Raiders' Dawn* and *Ha! Ha! Among the Trumpets* by Alun Lewis: Edward Arnold Ltd and Harcourt Brace Jovanovich, Inc.: *Abinger Harvest* by E. M. Forster; BBC Publications: *The Listener*; Mr Stephen Spender and the Longman Group Ltd for the British Council: *Poetry since 1939* (published in 1946); Professor Quentin Bell: the work of Julian Bell; The Bodley Head: *Collected Poems*, Volumes 1 and 2, by Roy Campbell; Cambridge University Press: *Scrutiny*; Mr C. Day Lewis, Jonathan Cape Ltd, The Hogarth Press Ltd and Harold Matson Company Inc.: *Collected Poems 1954*, copyright C. Day Lewis; Mr Robert Graves, Cassell & Co. and Collins-Knowlton-Wing Inc.: 'What Was That War Like, Sir?', published by Cassell in *The Crane Bag*, and Collins-Knowlton-Wing, Inc., copyright © 1960 by Robert Graves; Mr Robert Graves, Cassell & Co. and Collins-Knowlton-Wing, Inc.: 'To Lucia at Birth' and 'Spoils' (*Collected Poems 1965* published by Cassell), and Collins-Knowlton-Wing Inc., copyright © 1961 by Robert Graves; The Clarendon Press: *Modern Poetry: A Personal Essay* by Louis MacNeice; Curtis Brown Ltd.: Mr G. S. Fraser's Introduction to *The White Horseman* and Mr Christopher Isherwood's *Lions and Shadows*; Mr Harold Owen, Chatto & Windus Ltd and New Directions Publishing Corporation: *The Collected Poems of Wilfred Owen*; J. M. Dent & Sons Ltd and New Directions Publishing Corporation, the Trustees for the Copyrights of the late Dylan Thomas: *Collected Poems* by Dylan Thomas; J. M. Dent & Sons Ltd: *Poems 1935–48*; by Clifford Dyment; Mr Roy Fuller and André Deutsch Ltd: *Collected Poems 1936–1961*; Gerald Duckworth and Co. Ltd: *Collected Satires and Poems* by Osbert Sitwell; Mr W. H. Auden, Faber and Faber Ltd and Random House Inc.: *Age of Anxiety*, *Shield of Achilles* and *New Year Letter*; Faber and Faber Ltd and Chilmark Press Inc.: *Collected Poems* by Keith Douglas; Mr Gavin Muir, Faber and Faber Ltd and Oxford University Press, N.Y.: *Collected Poems 1921–1951* by Edwin Muir and *The Criterion* (published by Faber & Faber Ltd); Faber & Faber Ltd and Oxford University Press, N.Y.: *Poems* by Louis MacNeice; Faber & Faber Ltd and Horizon Press, N.Y.: *Collected Poems* by Sir Herbert Read, and copyright © 1966 by Horizon Press; Mr Stephen Spender, Faber and Faber Ltd, Hogarth Press and Random House Inc.: the author's work; Mr Charles Causley, Rupert Hart-Davis Ltd and Harold Ober Associates, N.Y.: *Survivor's Leave*; Mr Richard Church and William Heinemann Ltd: *Collected Poems* and *Twentieth Century Psalter*; The Executors of the Estate of Francis Brett Young, William Heinemann Ltd and A. Watkins Inc., N.Y.: *The Island*,

8 ACKNOWLEDGEMENTS

copyright © 1944 by Francis Brett Young; The Hogarth Press: *New Writing* and *New Writing and Daylight*; Lawrence & Wishart Ltd: *New Writing*; Mr John Lehmann and A. Watkins Inc.: *New Writing in Europe, The Whispering Gallery, The Age of the Dragon* and *Penguin New Writing*; David Higham Associates and Mr John Lehmann: *Shadow of Cain* by Edith Sitwell; the Trustees of the Hardy Estate, Macmillan & Co. Ltd, Macmillan and Company, New York, and The Macmillan Company of Canada: *The Dynasts* by Thomas Hardy; Macmillan & Co. Ltd and Macmillan and Company, New York: *Night Watch for England*, by Edward Shanks; David Higham Associates Ltd and Macmillan & Co. Ltd: *Street Songs* by Edith Sitwell; Professor Charles Madge: his poem, 'Letter to the Intelligentsia'; Mr Patric Dickinson and Methuen & Co. Ltd: *Stone in the Midst*; Mrs George Bambridge, Methuen & Co. Ltd and Doubleday & Company, Inc.: *The Years Between* by Rudyard Kipling; the *New Statesman*; Mr Christopher Fry and Oxford University Press: *A Sleep of Prisoners*; Mr David Gascoyne and Oxford University Press: *Collected Poems*: A. D. Peters & Company and the Harold Matson Company, Inc.: *Undertones of War*, copyright by Edmund Blunden; A. D. Peters and Company and the Harold Matson Company, Inc.: *World Within World*, and copyright © 1951 by Stephen Spender; Mr John Pudney and David Higham Associates Ltd: work published by John Lane The Bodley Head; Miss Kathleen Raine: an article in *New Road*, 1944; Routledge & Kegan Paul Ltd: *Collected Peoms* by Sidney Keyes, and the work of Alan Rook, Alex Comfort and Keidrych Rhys; The Literary Trustees of Walter de la Mare and the Society of Authors as their representative: *Motley* by Walter de la Mare; *The Spectator*. Mr Rex Warner and the Hogarth Press for excerpts from *New Country*.

Preface

THE reader of this book on war poetry may wonder why the poets of the First World War who have such a standing in present-day criticism, have been relegated such a small place here. It is precisely because they have been reviewed so frequently that I have chosen to concentrate on what followed 1914–18 rather than dwell too long on this well-mined area. It seemed to me that the approaches to the subject of war among the 'thirties poets was not an aspect that had been seen regularly in the light of 'war poetry' though its effects are strewn everywhere across their work. The latter became an interesting lead into the poetry of the Second World War, which is what I have mainly concentrated on.

This book does not pretend to sift or evaluate literary merit; it is assumed that the reader recognises where this may lie. It is an historical survey of a particular theme in the poetry of a period, and reference has been restricted to works which relate to this theme.

CHAPTER ONE

Introduction – Up to 1918

'My argument is that War makes rattling good history;
but Peace is poor reading. So I back Bonaparte for the
reason that he will give pleasure to posterity'.
(HARDY, *The Dynasts*)

IN the British Museum stands the famous black obelisk of
Shalmanezer III, King at Nimrud in the ninth century B.C.
It is decorated with a series of designs showing the tribute
paid to Shalmanezer as a result of his victories. A King
kneels, and oxen, camels, horses, apes and men bring their
gifts or are themselves led as gifts to the conquering hero.
The cuneiform writing that also decks the obelisk tells of
Shalmanezer's reign. He was King for thirty-five years
and for thirty-one of these he was engaged in war. The
whole monument is a tribute to the achievements of
war.

It is a small obelisk, about six feet high, but in shape it
resembles many of the cenotaphs which were erected in
this country after the First World War. Like them it was
designed to stand in a public place – in the street between
the palace and the temple at Nimrud – where people
might gaze, admire, and learn wisdom.

Perhaps nothing in the West so marks off the present
century from all previous centuries as the attitude of its
conscience towards war. The monuments which the country sprouted after 1918 are, unlike Shalmanezer's obelisk,
not reminders of triumph but read like gravestones,
lamenting the dead. They even, like gravestones, have that
little extra space beneath the inscription or on the other

side, which the next generation has dutifully filled in: For the Fallen 1939–45.

It is my intention in this book to examine another kind of memorial and to see how the work of poets reflects the theme of war in this century. Some poets writing from their immediate experience write of war because they are involved in it. Others who make a conscious attempt to reflect their times embody a war fever in their poetry because they see their time as a war age. Many of these poets (e.g. the 1930 poets) consider that since the age is one of shock and disruption it is their duty to say something to and for their contemporaries, so Shelley's poet-legislator comes to the fore. This book concerns itself mainly with the English literary scene and with those poets who reflect a war age.

If we go back to the beginning of the English scene, we shall find in its literature what I shall term the 'communal approach' to war. To the early English, the fight for survival was quite literal. The Anglo-Saxon period as reflected by its writers was an age not of war but of the warrior. It resembles the 'warrior' ages of other civilisations, e.g. the Gilgamesh, the Roman, etc., in its emphasis on strength, leadership, and bravery in battle. True enough it heroicises the nobleman because it was a court literature, but where the noble led, the people followed, and the spirit was a communal one. The poets expressed a whole people's outlook in their tales of contemporary events like Maldon or historical (usually biblical) warfare, even though it remained on a heroic level – they expressed an age that looked to its leaders to safeguard it. Battle itself was never tragic. It was life that was tragic, but in battle a man could triumph over life by dying bravely. The halls of the victorious dead awaited the warrior whose courage waxed in the face of defeat. War was not to be thought of as divorced from the ordinary run of everyday events, it was the terms on which men ran their society by sheer necessity. This is not to say that the Anglo-Saxon failed to recognise that war brought tragedy – the theme of loss and the sorrow of survivors is always uppermost in the poet's mind – but they accepted this as a natural part of life, for life was always a struggle.

Almost any Anglo-Saxon text gives the impression of the hardness of life. If we think of the English climate without any of our present means of heating, of the rawness of the winter, the early descent of unrelieved darkness, the tyranny of the sea over small manned craft, the division of the country into several centres that survived only according to their strength, the threat of invasion from abroad – we have the daily relentless background to the poet's description of nightly revels in the mead hall. The gathering of the community under the protection of its warriors was the only preservation against enemies and, as *Beowulf* indicates, against unknown terrors. The poet, without any debate on the matter, wrote as a member of a society, to express the ideals of that society.

Advance to the Middle Ages and war becomes less a social necessity than a social art. Together with knowing the elaborate code of chivalry went proficiency in handling deadly weapons. The element of Romance, epitomised in Chaucer's 'Knight's Tale' glossed over the fact that in reality war was barbaric. Any form of warfare that is regarded as an art and developed with the pleasure of art (in this case involving torture), carries its own contradiction. The Middle Ages attitude to war may well be compared with that of the Japanese during the Second World War.

In a literature that was written mainly for court circles, soldiering was still the hallmark of a gentleman, and the means of gaining personal honour and fame. In a feudal society the rank and file might expect little consideration. The predatory and self-preserving instincts of man had recourse to a system of feuds – between king and baron, between baron and baron, between members of a family fighting for inheritance. The leisure of the leisured classes was devoted to a training for violence. The code of chivalry allowed questions of moral right and wrong to be decided by single combat, a custom that survived in the form of duelling, and may be recognised today in the schoolboy's injunction to 'stand up and fight'.

The fighting tradition continued through the court literature of the Elizabethan period, through Sidney and Spenser. Because, when all was said and done, tales of battle were entertainment, as popular as the glorification of England and at times synonymous. But a new aspect of war penetrated the drama. The 'people's entertainment' had always tended to be realistic. Some of the scenes in Shakespeare's history plays were based on what was common knowledge among the lower classes of Elizabethan England, but had been missed out of the romanticised court literature. Henry V before Harfleur, Falstaff and his army of ragamuffins, Henry IV trying to avoid war for the preservation of his country, in *Henry VI* the tragedy of civil war in which a father has killed his son and a son has killed his father – the atrocities, the hardship, the innocent suffering, the scavengers, the disease, are some of the realities of war at least suggested, side by side with the chivalry. By recognising that war involved ordinary human beings and was not just waged by knights and heroes, it spoke for a hitherto neglected stratum of the population.

After that we have a significant lull, when the view of war becomes a matter personal to the poet. We hear that the Cavalier poet is on his way to war and must leave the beloved behind, and we know what Milton thought of gunpowder, but war was no longer expressed in literature as a popular part of the social structure or the social conscience. Milton pursued the epic ideal as a literary form and the latter part of the seventeenth century witnessed the mammoth production of the heroic drama, but the age of heroes had disappeared. Civil War was part of, and contributed to, the sense of disruption, of an old order changing. The greatest blessing it could bring was not victory but peace, and the seventeenth-century poet was remarkably silent on the subject. The expression of an age of which the war itself was merely an outcome, was what occupied most of the main writers of the time.

The period that emerged from the trauma of civil war was one in which soldiering (if we disregard the brutal practice of impress for the rank and file) was less a necessity than a career, and the poet chose to stay at home. The wars of the age were merely the background to the age, and Dryden could sit in a boat politely discussing with three other gentlemen whether to rhyme or not to rhyme, to the noise of guns a little farther off down the Channel.

Most of the eighteenth century followed in much the same way. The new nation of shopkeepers still needed its protectors but it was a very convenient thing that most of the fighting was taking place on foreign soil. George II was the last Hanoverian martial leader. The new office of Prime Minister that emerged with Walpole was purely civilian. Poetry was still the occupation of the gentleman, and the poet was more interested in the social world at home than in the everlasting conflict abroad. Where the subject did occur, it was in the form of England's part in war, a social celebration of her success in a poem like 'Annus Mirabilis'.

With the Romantics an interest in the European situation again invaded the world of letters. This time the poet was writing as an individual, not as the voice of society. The attitude was therefore varied and changeable. The French Revolution for instance, made an immediate but short-lived appeal to Wordsworth. The ideal of liberty was very much to the fore in the work of Wordsworth, Byron, and Shelley, and it seemed that the world was in a state where liberty had to be fought for. But the attitude

towards England's part in previous and present wars was
one of disillusionment. Southey's 'After Blenheim', and
Byron's 'Childe Harold' mention the waste and fruitless-
ness of war, or perhaps it would be more correct to say –
of particular wars. Byron was only too ready to go and
fight for Greek independence when he thought that fighting could accomplish something in the future. But where
England's efforts in the past are concerned

> What good came of it at last?

asks little Peterkin about Marlborough's famous victory.
And in Byron's well-known stanzas on Waterloo we find
the bitterness of a modern attitude to war – the revolutionary ardour dissolving into the cynical knowledge that
war accomplishes nothing except to leave behind it a fine
memorial:

> Stop! – for thy tread is on an Empire's dust!
> An Earthquake's spoil is sepulchred below!
> Is the spot mark'd with no colossal bust?
> Nor column trophied for triumphal show?
> None; but the morals' truth tells simpler so,
> As the ground was before, thus let it be; –
> How that red rain hath made the harvest grow!
> And is this all the world hath gain'd by thee,
> Thou first and last of fields! king-making Victory?

But war is still divorced from the rest of life, the poet
from the soldier, the sympathy from the pity. Even the
cynicism makes 'rattling good history' with its

> Rider and horse, – friend, foe, – in one red burial blent.

The nineteenth century continued the romanticising. Few
poems contain more of the excitement traditionally associated with war than 'The Charge of the Light Brigade',
though at the same time this is a serious piece of criticism
of the British command in the Crimea.

Francis Brett Young's 'The Island' was a poem produced during the Second World War, reviewing England's past history and battles, designed to show the pluck of our forefathers in situations which seemed as rough as ours, and how everything has led up to Britain's 'finest hour'. In dealing with historical episodes the poet has tried to capture some of the different ways in which men thought at different times and their various attitudes to war. The 'Episode of the Garrulous Centurion', for instance, bears out our conclusion on the Roman period:

> Of course we had fighting
> Now and again; but war is a soldier's duty,
> And fighting's what he's paid for.

Now listen to the 'Elegy in Whitehall November 11th 1920'. Here the poet captures the sudden change the First World War brought to men's outlook. Here is the bitterness which not even the 1939 conflict could equal, and the turning-point in the poem's theme:

> There was an age when feckless poets sought
> Vicarious raptures in the clash of swords;
> Nay, even in war's hideous features traced
> A baleful splendour. Tell not us who fought
> With Prussia's brutish hordes
> That war breeds aught but butchery and waste.
> Spare us your threadbare cant of chivalry:
> War is no princely sport
> But a fool's game in which Death loads the die:
> So speak the truth for our dead comrades' sakes –
> War maims and kills more heroes than it makes.

I think it would be true to say that here in English letters is an outlook – anti-heroic, anti-myth – which because it appears substantially for the first time during the 1914–18 conflict and is confirmed not only by the 1939–45 war but by every anti-Vietnam, anti-Imperialist, anti-nuclear demonstration that takes place, by every breath that is breathed on the subject of organised strife

(whatever the practice may be), has come to be regarded
as a twentieth-century phenomenon.

I have not the smallest doubt that the final sentiment
expressed in that quotation from 'The Island' has been
experienced by the small and insignificant on occasions of
battle down the ages. We hear from time to time of
monarchs like Alfred the Great whose ideas ran so counter
to the tenor of their times that they considered some of the
arts of peace superior to and morally more uplifting for
man than the arts of war. But the relegation of learning
and even simple literacy to a chosen class of people has
until this century prevented the voice being heard of the
ninety-nine per cent mass of the population whose blood
has fed history's battle fields. The universal propagation
of at least elementary education, plus conscription,
brought by 1916 not only the poets into the trenches but
poets drawn from a new stratum of the population, who
were aligned with the common man and expressed the
view of the common man, and who understood more
readily the common man's desire to save his skin and to
achieve the life which for his class was reaching at last a
standard that promised some comfort in a future on this
earth. At the same time, as the poet stood shoulder to
shoulder with the ordinary fighting man, he found himself
not just on the opposite side of the line from the enemy
but drawn up in a very closely packed rank of living and
(as time went on) of dead, against the establishment that
had placed him in a situation of war. The great voices of
the 1914 conflict express a comradeship of soldiers, of
men, of human beings, both English and German, against
their own politicians. The war is marked by anger at the
authorities. 'This book is not about heroes. English Poetry
is not yet fit to speak of them. . . . these elegies are to
this generation in no sense consolatory,' wrote Wilfred
Owen.

Like the 'Anthem for Doomed Youth' many of his

poems are characterised by a white heat of anger whose
expression is merely parodied by 'the monstrous anger of
the guns', relieved in the end by the very source of the
anger, the indescribable pity of it. There runs through his
poetry that timeless frustration that such things can be,
that what is done cannot be undone, and yet what is done
is to no purpose:

> The sun may cleanse,
> And time, and starlight. Life will sing sweet songs,
> And gods will show us pleasures more than men's.
> But the old Happiness is unreturning.
> Boy's griefs are not so grievous as youth's yearning,
> Boys have no sadness sadder than our hope.

Almost every one of Owen's war poems gains its impact
by that simple swing of the pendulum between those very
large, simple emotions, anger and pity. They supply a
rhythm of feeling as we move between them, they come
together and take their peculiar vigour one from the other
like Siamese twins. For some readers the combination has
been too painful. For others, like Yeats, it has too
theatrically lit up the subject matter, turning the grim
details into Gothic.

Owen's poetry is without doubt romantic to the present
generation of readers. But what differentiates it and the
best of the First World War poetry generally from what
had gone before is the reality of the situation in which it is
created, and which it reflects. The simple and sincere lyric
carrying the expression of the individual man is characteristic of twentieth-century war poetry. Perhaps Owen's use
on the one hand of the Georgian stock-in-trade when he
writes of starlight and life singing sweet songs and the old
Happiness and the Boys and youth's yearning, makes
strange bedfellows with that more physical realism of
desecrated flesh and blood, limbs and broken bodies that
became his own particular stock-in-trade, yet these are

merely channels to convey events that were in the end
larger than his art. 'I am not concerned with Poetry. . . .
The Poetry is in the pity.'

The emphasis on mutilation and physical conditions is
more an aspect of First World War poetry than it is of
Second World War poetry, as also is the desire on the part
of the poet to shock. The two things go hand in hand. The
reasons for this aren't hard to find. First of all the war
itself came as a shock to the men who in the first flush of
epic gallantry enlisted or who later were conscripted. It
was something new in the way of pointless and degrading
suffering.

There had been almost a century of peace. The Boer
War and the Crimean were too distant and isolated to
have an effect on many except those who fought in them
or were on the scene. They were after all in pursuance of
the old ideal of British mastery while at the same time producing a whole stock of famous names (Nightingale,
Kitchener, Gordon), all indicative of the famous bulldog
spirit and sufficient for the British public to wave its flags
over.

How unexpected the First World War was in its effect
can be seen from the kind of poetry that heralded its outbreak. The heroic ideals that poured from poets like
Brooke and Grenfell are too well known for me to dwell on
them. That magnificent paean, 'Into Battle', stands on the
threshold of a new age, looking only in the direction of the
past. Or perhaps the present is in it too, for it is born of
Edwardian peace and green unspoiled English lawns and
endless summers. The war horses are pawing the ground
with eagerness, for they are well rested.

Yet something creeps in. As early as 1914 even a poet
like Kipling senses the change. He writes in 'For all we
have and are',

> Our world has passed away,
> In wantonness o'erthrown,

> There is nothing left today
> But steel and fire and stone.

Then came the trenches, and the lice, and the gas, and the shells, and the dead – everywhere the dead. We have to remember that it was possible to live for months in these conditions. The pressures may have been no less in the more mechanised 1939 conflict, but they were different. George Orwell has given us in his *Homage to Catalonia* a vivid description of life under siege during the Spanish Civil War. What it is like to be contained in a world of lice and rats that you can't get away from and that increase as the dead also increase.

The result in First World War poetry was a conception of the soldier in his comparative innocence, helplessness and pain, as a martyred saviour. 'Gethsemane 1914–18' is typical. Here the poet records his meeting with gas during the war as the epitome of all human suffering and the cup which a man prays might pass from him.

War itself is seen almost entirely as a destroying agent. It destroys the physical form, it destroys through death the comradeships it has brought into being, and it destroys that which might have been. With regard to the poet himself this is seen as involving the destruction of his own gift, the poetic power:

> I would have poured my spirit without stint
> But not through wounds; not on the cess of war.

Suddenly when the old battle ideals of honour and chivalry, and the home-front patriotism, had become dead-sea fruit, the poet discovers a new task:

> We shall sing to you
> Of the men who have been trampled
> To death in the circus of Flanders.
>
> . . . .
>
> You hope that we shall tell you that they found their
> happiness in fighting,

Or that they died with a song on their lips,
Or that we shall use the old familiar phrases
With which your paid servants please you in the press:
But we are poets,
And shall tell the truth.

('Rhapsode', Osbert Sitwell)

The First World War did two things for the poets themselves. It made them think about war as divorced from
time and events, war in the abstract, what it does for and
against civilisation. And it gave them a purpose in their
writing. 'All a poet can do today is warn. That is why the
true Poets must be truthful,' wrote Owen. Over and over
again the poet sets himself the task of reflecting the age to
the age, partly because the men who went out to fight were
so divorced from the civilians who stayed at home. Later
on Hitler and the Luftwaffe not only evened out the area
of suffering, but changed the need for one half of a country in arms to understand the other half, to the need for a
whole nation to understand the same experience.

Herbert Read tells in an ode, 'Written during the battle
of Dunkirk, May, 1940', of his experience of coming
through the First World War:

One of the dazed and disinherited
I crawled out of that mess
with two medals and a gift of blood-money.
No visible wounds to lick – only a resolve
to tell the truth without rhetoric
the truth about war and about men
involved in the indignities of war.

In those poets of pronounced sensibility, like Owen,
there is an interesting tension achieved between material
that is in itself repulsive, and the natural craving for as
well as the Romantic belief in the beautiful. In the end
there must be the re-creation of war and its horrors in the
terms of art. The reaction of a mind responding to the

youthful delights of the world more sharply than most is summed up in Osbert Sitwell's 'The Poet's Lament' that prefaces his *Poems of the Last and the Next War* (1931). He tells us there:

> Before the dawning of the death-day
> My mind was a confusion of beauty.
> Thoughts fell from it in riot
> Of colour,
> In wreaths and garlands of flowers and fruit. . . .
>
> Then the red dawn came
> – And no thought touched me
> Except pity, anger
> And bitter reproach.

Later, in an essay on 'Wilfred Owen', Sitwell wrote:

> the very phrase War Poet indicates a strange twentieth-century phenomenon, the attempt to combine two incompatibles. There had been no War Poets in the Peninsular, Crimean, or the Boer Wars. But War had suddenly become transformed by the effort of scientist and mechanician into something so infernal, so inhuman, that it was recognised that only their natural enemy, the poet, could pierce through the armour of horror with which they were encased to the pity at the human core; only the poet could steadily contemplate the struggle at the level of tragedy. . . .[1]

There were certain poets who chose deliberately to opt out of taking war as a theme for their verse, though they were more likely to be poets not involved in the fighting. Where much poetry, however, bears no witness to the external events of the war, it still echoes a dissonant world. Walter de la Mare for instance has written only an occasional poem dealing with the subject. But however he might choose to turn from war's grimness, he is as much aware of it as Jane Austen no doubt was of Waterloo:

[1] Penguin *New Writing* 27, 1946.

Nay but a dream I had
Of a world all mad.
Not simple happy mad like me,
Who am mad like an empty scene
Of water and willow tree,
Where the wind hath been.[1]

Of the major poets of the period, neither Yeats nor Eliot has chosen to produce 'war poetry'. Perhaps in the end when our age is past this will reduce war to a very small devil and press the final seal of twentieth-century contempt on the 'fighting hero'. When Yeats was asked to produce a war poem he stated that in such times it was better for the poet to remain silent, and E. M. Forster has told us in *Abinger Harvest* of how, during the First World War when stationed in India, he came across the work of T. S. Eliot, and how he was affected by the poet's disgust at tea parties:

> For what, in that world of gigantic horror, was tolerable except the slighter gestures of dissent? He who measured himself against the war, who drew himself to his full height, as it were, and said to Armadillo-Armageddon 'Avaunt!' collapsed at once into a pinch of dust. But he who could turn aside to complain of ladies and drawing-rooms preserved a tiny drop of our self-respect, he carried on the human heritage.

[1] 'Motley'.

CHAPTER TWO

The 1930 Poets

THE 'war' poetry that was produced in the decade immediately following the First World War is not of any great significance. The voice of T. S. Eliot dominated the literary scene and the emphasis was on the development of a new kind of poetry. Apart from this the poets who emerged from the conflict, with the exception of Sassoon, were not its major exponents, nor did their poetry express the same immediacy after the event as that produced during the war had done. The poems remain merely a comment, a reflection, on something that is past. Where it becomes of more interest is when that tendency to look back on the past is brought into contact with a direct renewal of similar events when the Second World War broke out. I have therefore left discussion of the 'survivors'' work until later in this book, when the attitude of poets like Herbert Read, Edmund Blunden, Richard Church, and Robert Graves will be considered as a lead into the later war poetry and when we can gain perspective by a contrast of an older generation of writers with the new soldier poets.

Where war and strife do resume a new immediacy is early in the 1930 decade, culminating in 1936 with the Spanish Civil War. The 1930 poets are in fact more directly the outcome of the First World War than are the writers of the 1920s. Day Lewis's *A Hope for Poetry*, produced in 1934, mentioned Owen as one of the literary forebears of the poetic movement, and there was among these poets of what I shall later allude to as the middle generation, a harking back to the influences of childhood.

That childhood had been passed during the Great War. Therefore war thoughts and war impressions never ceased to haunt them. Christopher Isherwood in his autobiography *Lions and Shadows*, wrote in 1938: 'We young writers of the middle twenties were all suffering, more or less subconsciously, from a feeling of shame that we hadn't been old enough to take part in the European war.' Again Michael Roberts in his Preface to *New Country* in 1933 points out how the young poets of his generation have never really known what it is to be free from the shadow of war, they had been brought up to be 'Sergeants of our school O.T.C.s, admirers of our elder brothers'.

As a result of the fashionable Freudian habit of psychoanalysis, we find at this period a willingness in most writers to pry into the subconscious reasons for disappointment, frustration, and the timeless melancholia – and continually the blame is laid at the door of war. The oddness which these writers seem to have liked finding not only in themselves but in their fellow writers – *Lions and Shadows* and Spender's *World within a world*, for instance, are full of caricatures where Auden, 'Chalmers', Spender, and Isherwood are concerned – this oddness time and again was balanced by a search for some communal cause: war, public-school life, Cambridge, Fascism, propaganda, Communist lack of compromise, and above all from a society that had lost all contact between poet and ordinary reader. In connection with war, Isherwood wrote:

> Like most of my generation, I was obsessed by a complex of terrors and longings connected with the idea 'War'. 'War' in this purely neurotic sense, meant The Test. The test of your courage, of your maturity, of your sexual prowess: 'Are you really a Man?'[1]

But the war atmosphere was not merely an extension of neurotic sensibility. The 'war to end wars' had put almost

[1] *Lions and Shadows.*

every European country on the defensive, the development of the cinema and the increasing tendency to travel abroad created greater awareness of what was taking place. As Julian Bell wrote in his satire *Arms and the Man*:

> Russia's a threat – by being on the map –
> Or how can France her million men resign
> While fifty thousand Germans threat the Rhine?[1]

And John Lehmann in the same volume, sees

> The Modern World divided into nations:
> So neatly planned, that if you merely tap it
> The armaments will start their devastations,
> . . . .
> And very few are asking Why not scrap it?[2]

The 1930s in England saw a general movement among poets to become Left-Wing supporters in the field of politics, and their names were connected with Communism. The sense of a new movement emerging was fostered by their grouping themselves together, taking a common stand, and contributing to periodicals that were founded with the intention of bringing their views to the public. So there came into being *New Signatures* (1932), *New Country* (1933), *New Writing* (1936–8). John Lehmann afterwards wrote of the birth of *New Writing*:

> as soon as Hitler triumphed in Berlin and the terrible stream of refugees began to pour over the world, this intellectual interchange between the artists and the anti-Fascist political groupings became even closer. I realised that this was beginning to create a literature with special qualities of its own, and a powerful realistic and human appeal.[3]

[1] *New Signatures*, 1932.
[2] 'This Excellent Machine'.
[3] *New Writing in Europe*, New York, 1940.

I should emphasise that it was not only poets who were affected by this move towards intellectual political consolidation, but it was a movement that sought to take in both intellectuals of any sphere and men who stood for the 'workers' of society as much as for the 'writers'. What is important is that the poets were part of the scheme. The poetic outlook of the 1920s, the spiritual disillusionment confining itself self-consciously in Eliot's work to a world of art, was being changed to a poetic participation in social and political ideologies. The atmosphere was therefore a new one. After the despair and disillusionment of the previous decade, there was new vigour, a hope of new vistas, an urge to change the present state of affairs: Rex Warner in his 'Hymn' in *New Country*, calls for a renewal of youth:

> Come, then, companions. This is the spring of blood,
> heart's hey-day, movement of masses, beginning of good.

It is significant that the periodicals produced during this period emphasise the term 'new' in their titles. The major poets we associate with this period, however different their poetic talent may be – I allude of course to the Auden–Spender–Day Lewis–MacNeice group – all emphasise the turn poetry has taken and the commitment of the poet to a community at large. As Arthur Calder-Marshall later wrote: 'There was never a decade in which so large a body of dissident writers felt enough unity to refer to themselves in the first person plural.'[1]

The atmosphere itself was full of impending action. It might in part have been a reaction to the previous decade, to the economic depression, the queues waiting for the dole, the noise of the military machine on the Continent. But more than anything it was the result of that impetus given to thought and ideals by the Russian Revolution. It took some time for the full impact to reach England, but

[1] *New Statesman*, February 15th 1941.

the revolutionary interest seeped its way through the 1920 decade. Michael Roberts wrote of how, after the First World War, we lost all sense of security, feeling that the world was in nobody's hands: 'Politics isn't, and hasn't been, a real activity in our time.'[1] Now the taking of sides is seen as the necessary task of the intellectual, and this inevitably meant the involvement of the poet.

Many people have since asked if the 1930 writers had anything more than a naïve grasp on Communism as a system to live under. Some, like Spender and Auden, turned to the Left-Wing partly because they had seen the dangers of Fascism in Germany. Though a later reviewer wrote scathingly of their 'first-hand experience':

> The pattern of the growth of Fascism, which obsessed the work of the 'thirties', was an intellectual formula, evolved by schoolmasters who knew no Fascists or Communists, no armament manufacturers or international gunmen . . . and when Auden and Isherwood were commissioned to report the Chinese war, they produced a book which Nero would have enjoyed reading while Rome burnt.[2]

Nevertheless, to most writers of the time, the definiteness of Communism as a system of beliefs realisable in practical terms was an incentive to a new beginning. As in many Anglo-Saxon battles just before the end – hope was renewed. C. Day Lewis's *The Magnetic Mountain* is a rallying call, a paean of joy, a looking forward with expectation —

> Broad let our valleys embrace the morning
> And satisfied see a good day dying,
> Accepting the shadows, sure of seed.

Spender in *New Signatures* calls

[1] Preface to *New Country*, 1933.
[2] *New Statesman*, February 15th, 1941.

> Oh comrades step beautifully from the solid wall
> advance to rebuild, and sleep with friend on hill.[1]

There was so much to rebuild – that was the crux of the matter. It was little wonder that in the depression of post-war years Communism should become popular – in blunt headlines of equality and a fair handing out to the worker of that which he had worked for, it couldn't fail to appeal. As always lesser writers are inclined to reflect the age directly, to deal with the details that make up an ordinary man's dissatisfaction with life – so Julian Bell writes sarcastically of England's economic depression:

> Long queues of unemployed th'Exchange besiege,
> And that's all right, because of our Prestige.[2]

And Rex Warner —

> Nothing keen in us workless, us almost crying,
> dogged, dazed, rebellious, cranked, taut or tied,
> who have lost the smile of the wind, the fierce heart, the
> glad heart and the easy stride.[3]

Not only in these writers, but throughout *The Magnetic Mountain*, we have emphasised the fact that 'the old order changeth, yielding place to new' – that the old world has ceased to satisfy:

> Geared too high our power was wasted,
> Who have lost the old way to the happy ending.

The time has now come to strike because the fight has begun a long time before England is forced to enter active conflict, the whole age being reflected in the poet's mind as one of struggle.

> It is now or never, the hour of the knife,
> The break with the past, the major operation,

[1] 'Oh Young Men'.
[2] 'Arms and the Man' (*New Signatures*).
[3] Chorus from 'The Dam' (*New Country*).

In his 'Letter to a Young Revolutionary' Day Lewis emphasises Auden's view – that England is sick – and suggests that what is wanted is not just a new economic system, but a new heart – the task of the revolutionary is to cultivate in the Englishman 'the seeds of courage, jollity, truth and self-respect'.

Even allowing for the tidal wave of popular enthusiasm, we might still wonder why poets should seize so thoroughly upon Communism and make it a rallying-point for their art. Charles Madge, in his 'Letter to the Intelligentsia' is writing party propaganda:

> Lenin, would you were living at this hour.

ending with a plea to the English to join the team and become part of a world complex:

> we turn the pages
> Of a larger atlas; telegrams come in
> From China, and the world is mapped on our brains
> Rainbow from cell to cell.[1]

Auden in 'A Communist to Others' writes from a similar point of view. Yet most writers had no practical experience of the working of Communism – the behaviour of Communists in the Spanish Civil War brought disillusionment to many who came into contact with them. On occasion we see the poets themselves being cautious in their ignorance. Day Lewis, for instance, insisted in his 'Letter to a Young Revolutionary' that of course the way Communism worked in Russia could not be expected to succeed in England.

But the leaning of the thirties' poets towards the ideals of a classless society had deep roots in their thinking about art, the art of poetry in particular. It was after all the poet above any who was at a distance from the public he craved for. Communism could well be a political means to a

---

[1] *New Country*, 1933.

literary end. The very journey towards that end seemed to be enlarging the circle of people who might read and be interested in a verse that was seeking to reflect its age and embody the up-to-date ideals of that age, in its very contemporaneity in fact. Herbert Read, although not in support of the totalitarian government that Russia had provided herself with, sees in *Poetry and Anarchism* (1938) that an 'essential Communism' is needed to provide the classless society where art can flourish —

> it is almost impossible to be a poet in an industrial age, nor is it possible for art to flourish where there is no suitable relationship between an individual and society. In the classless society, the mind of every individual will have at least the opportunity to expand in breadth and depth, and culture will once more be the natural product of economic circumstances.

There was a spate of writing on this particular subject. Michael Roberts earlier raised the flag against 'the commercialisation of culture', and informed the intelligentsia that it could no longer remain aloof from politics:

> It is time that those who would conserve something which is still valuable in England began to see that only a revolution can save their standards. It's past the stage of sentimental pity for the poor, we're all in the same boat . . . Provincial life is impoverished and the intellectual is turned to a pettifogging squabbler in Bloomsbury drawing-rooms or a recluse 'in country houses at the end of drives'.[1]

In effect, Eliot's warning against measuring out life in coffee spoons was being taken seriously by the next generation.

Spender in his essay 'Poetry and Revolution' points out that the artist is bound by a bourgeois audience – nothing new can be produced in that tradition, and there is no

[1] *New Country*, 1933.

hope of an audience outside it. Therefore: 'For these reasons he is tempted to feel that the artist should go into politics now as there is no need for art.'[1] In a later work Spender insists – like Read – that the artist should not be a politician, but since a special kind of society is required for the development and freedom of the imagination, the artist must have an interest in the state, he must find a way between the armoured tank and the ivory tower. At the same time Spender also suggests, looking back on it, a reason for the failure of the 'Pink Decade' of the '30s:

> We were in a false position. Hypnotised by the sense of the necessity of saving civilisation from fascism, we were entangled in a net of theoretical ways and means which evaded our grasp . . . These writers, artists, scientists, supported the politics which seemed to offer the one chance of saving their disinterested and civilising activities. But the intellectual, having given politics his support, became an Orestes pursued by Furies of Ends and Means, Propaganda and Necessity.[2]

The fact that it is the poet's duty to join in the struggle and take sides emerges frequently in the poetry. In *The Magnetic Mountain*, the fourth enemy tempts the writer:

> You're a poet, so am I:
> No man's keeper, intimate
> Of breeding earth and brooding sky,
> Irresponsible, remote –
> A cool cloud, creation's eye.
> Seek not to turn the winter tide
> But to temperate deserts fly.

But the poet's reply has a stern and irrevocable temper:

> Tempt me no more.

[1] *New Country*, 1933.
[2] *Life and the Poet*.

C

The poet has a hard but necessary task:

> Bayonets are closing round.
> I shrink; yet I must wring
> A living from despair
> And out of steel a song.

When these poets got round to the actual fighting of the Spanish Civil War, they had already been through a period of revolution. In some respects the poetry produced on the war hardly reflects the sense of struggle so well as that produced just before.

It was a movement in which poets were urging forward a future whose real consequences we know, looking back, they were blissfully unconscious of. Their work both possessed and lacked the characteristics of war. In the first place, it was clean and bloodless – its imagery consisted of spies, barriers, frontiers, leaders, even of the no-man's-land of 1914 memory – but not of the real physical hardships of war. There is at times a public school atmosphere of 'Play up, play up, and play the game'. It fostered the sense of comradeship, with the poet as one of the band, but it relied on singleness of purpose and faith in forging a new heaven and new earth. C. Day Lewis perhaps had more of the spirit of the movement than any other poet. In 'Learning to Talk'[1] he gives the rallying call:

> Though we fall once, though we often,
> Though we fall to rise not again,
> From our horizon sons begin;
> When we go down, they will be tall ones.

Comradeship did not exist through the pity or terror or shame Owen and Sassoon had previously distilled from war, although love is emphasised in a poet like Spender. But its heroics are now of a different calibre.

---

[1] *A Time to Dance.*

Bravery is now
Not in the dying breath
But resisting the temptations
To sky-line operations.[1]

Day Lewis's 'Letter to a Young Revolutionary' asks:
'Have you the courage not to be a hero?' All the usual
feelings connected with war must be handed in like
weapons to a common depot, then revised and reissued.
All our efforts must aim at producing 'The integral spirit
and the communal sense'. The prayer of *The Magnetic
Mountain* is not that we might be spared pain in the new
Utopia – 'But that we may be given the chance to be
men.' It is a discipline that will make 'a depth-charge of
grief', and allow us to pass 'Alive into the house'. We
should notice the strangeness of this 'warfare' as typical of
a period that felt the strain – all the mental suffering without the physical activity to relieve it – the secrecy and at
the same time the shouting aloud that it must be kept
secret.[2]

The patriotic theme is by no means missing. Day Lewis
spoke directly to 'You that love England', and Madge
looked back on his time spent there with sentiments that it
is the habit nowadays to attribute discreditingly to Brooke:

Yes, England, I was at school with you, I've known
Your hills come open to me, call me crying
With bird voice.[3]

But England does not stand as an image of freedom –
rather is she connected with sickness and imprisonment,
assumed deliberately as an image of the post-war years of
hardship, the former being the impression Auden handed

[1] W. H. Auden, 'Missing' (*Poems*), 1930.
[2] A fine comic example of the deception and counter-deception
continental society had devised for itself can be found in Isherwood's *Mr. Norris Changes Trains*. (1935).
[3] 'Letter to the Intelligentsia' (*New Country*).

on to his followers, the latter expressed usually by out-and-out enthusiasts of Communism, with sentiments that recall those of Wordsworth gazing from afar at the French Revolution:

> Lenin, would you were living at this hour:
> England has need of you. . . .[1]

What we must see in these early years of the 1930s is a build-up of enthusiasm for the reform of society, but a reform that is viewed in terms of a campaign which allows expression to the war fever that the 1914–18 conflict had left as a legacy and which the young intellectuals could see was having more practical and sinister effects on the continent. I think on one level it was a furthering of the cause that Owen had taken up when he announced his intention of using his art on behalf of those who for centuries had lived to provide fodder for the military machine. The comrades who died like cattle were receiving a new justice in the defence of the proletariat. It was Marxist doctrine, of course. But the hold which a new doctrine takes upon a society has frequently been the outcome of war. The First World War wreaked such havoc, not only on the years 1914–18 but on the years that followed, that peace alone became inadequate as a recompense. The poetic movement stolidly proclaimed Marxist doctrine:

> a world where the will of all shall be raised to highest power,
> Village or factory shall form the unit.[2]

and at the same time many lesser names belonging to the movement were deliberately drawn by the men in charge from the working classes. Even if the authors belonged to the wrong class, the right subject matter was strictly adhered to. John Lehmann, speaking of *New Writing* tells us:

[1] 'Letter to the Intelligensia' (*New Country*).
[2] *The Magnetic Mountain.*

In No. 2, which appeared in the autumn of 1936, there were, for instance, contributors who had been leather-workers, plasterers, dock-labourers, seamen, wood-cutters, and tailors' apprentices, and among the themes chosen by the authors represented in No. 3, to take another instance, were miners at work in their pits, and miners wasting in unemployment, volunteers gathering in Paris for the International Brigade, workers fighting in Spain, homesick peasants struggling for a living in Burmese tea-plantations, peasants harvesting in France ... etc.

We cannot say though that we have any clear impression of what Communism was expected to accomplish, from the poetry. A little of what being a Communist might entail spiritually is found most clearly in Auden, who gives us a picture of the self-repression and resignation demanded in 'Missing' and 'The Secret Agent'.

But on the whole, 'the cause' is usually represented by allegory – in *The Magnetic Mountain* there is the setting out for a new country by rail, the mountain itself lying at the end of the journey, and the difficulty involved because

> No line is laid so far.
> Ties rusting in a stack
> And sleepers – dead men's bones –
> Mark a defeated track.

Perhaps this allegory is used because the form this pioneering is to take is never quite clear. It was not until the Spanish Civil War that any outlet for action was provided, though the immediate surge forward once it had broken out may in part be accounted for by the build-up of a 'side' during the years preceding.

Auden in a poem like 'Which side am I supposed to be on?'[1] impresses upon us the readiness and training for

[1] The Orators, 1934.

battle, the enemies summoning their hatred and envisaging the flight of the other, telling themselves which side God is on, and yet the sense that war is not yet come. All the military orders are there, the military machine, and the military regimentation – rather, we might imagine, like the school O.T.C.'s, but of signs of actual fighting there are none.

But the message of the First World War that war itself is an evil had not been entirely overlooked. Julian Bell is a poet-journalist with a steady eye on contemporary events and the realisation that another war is possible. He is inclined to despise the heroics that will lead to actual fighting:

> Yet, though for King and Country once men bled,
> What use are either to a man that's dead.[1]

Yet we should note the career of Julian Bell. The 1930s saw both the Resolution of the Oxford Union and the Peace Ballot, both declaring against war. In 1935 appeared a book edited by Bell, *We did not fight*, which contained experiences of pacifists from 1914–18. The Foreword tell us: 'There are now fifty thousand Englishmen pledged never to take part in another war.'[2] Julian Bell was one of these pacifists, and although it is only a small percentage of his work that reveals that fact, we must remember that he was really only at the start of his career. In a letter to Day Lewis he criticised the Communist Movement and the Marxist attitude, showing himself to be remarkably percipient about some of its supporters:

> it is a humanitarian, romantic attitude, at heart like a child of nineteenth century liberalism . . . it has its origins in the uneasiness of converts from the

[1] 'Arms and the Man' (*New Signatures*).
[2] Canon H. R. L. Sheppard.

bourgeoisie and in the bitterness and even more the snobbery of *déclassé* proletarians become intellectuals.

Later, Bell fought and died in the Spanish Civil War, not because he had changed his mind about pacifism, but because 'I believe that the war-resistance movements of my generation will in the end succeed in putting down war – by force if necessary.'[1]

The Spanish Civil War was the outlet for many hopes and fears concerning the poet's own generation, and the desire to establish peace was only one of them. Bell is an example of both the idealism and the seriousness of his times. The last statement of his quoted above reflects the paradox haunting the generation that had been just too young to fight in the Great War.

The 1930 writers above everything took their ideals seriously. They had a firm belief that it was possible to change the state they lived in, in turn establishing new values to replace the 'petty bourgeois of the soul'. Being determined to do something with his age, the poet was forced in the content of his poetry to take that age into account. The Introduction to *Poems for Spain* (1939) laid down, almost as a poetic principle reminiscent of 'Lyrical Ballads', that 'an understanding of the fundamental nature of political ideas' is 'a subject worthy of poetry'.

[1] Introduction to *We did not fight*.

CHAPTER THREE

The Spanish Civil War

WHEN in 1936 war came, and revolution, and the opportunity to hit at the hated powers of Fascism, there was hardly a young writer left unaffected by the event. As a pointer to what was to culminate in 1939 the Spanish Civil War was probably the most important event of the century. The sides were already formed for the great conflict and already at loggerheads, Europe was split into two camps, Russia had naturally come down on the side of the Spanish 'socialist' government, and Americans and British were drifting into the International Brigade. The European pact of neutrality kept Britain effectively out of the war as a country, though it had very little effect on the rest of Europe. As Churchill euphemistically phrased it on looking back on the war, France had been neutral and Britain had been strictly neutral. But it meant that British idealists who chose to support the Spanish Government against Franco did so as a matter of principle, not necessity.

The mixture of ingredients that composed the fight – revolution, civil war, international strife, struggle of political ideologies for supremacy, and even a Catholic Crusade, is only equalled by the number of things the Spanish War actually meant to those outside it. We have only to look at Day Lewis's 'Nabara' to realise that Spain was to those steeped in English traditions still a magic word that carried with it old heroic themes and battles long ago. And yet, to many who approached the war with high hopes, with an intellectual faith in an essential Communism for instance, it was their moment of disillusionment. Spender, who performed his part in a series of miscellaneous and rather undistinguished adventures while attending a writers' conference, tells us in his autobiography of those details that were the turning-point – the intractability of the Communists, the failure of any system of free thought, the selfishness of most of those concerned.

After the Second World War it is difficult for us to view the Spanish conflict as anything more than a pinprick. But for the young writers of the time it supplied the call to what Isherwood had summed up as 'the test of manhood'. They made it the rallying ground on which to fight for all the heroic qualities the century had either starved with poverty and unemployment, swamped in mass production, or failed to inspire in a commercialised civilisation.

> 'See Spain and see the world. Freedom extends
> or contracts in all hearts.'[1]

The Spanish conflict was the centre and the outlet for all the 'war' thoughts and aspirations that had been built up in the 1930s. But just as it was the training-ground for Mussolini's planes and armies it was the training-ground also for the hatred war sharpens and the bitterness it brings. At the same time there were those who went out to fight and to die like heroes. Clive Branson even in the prison camp of San Pedro sees the other prisoners as

> giants chained down from the skies
> To congregate an old and empty hell.[2]

What is most striking about the attitude of those who were willing to go and fight on foreign soil is their sense of the inevitability of whatever doom awaited them in Spain. John Cornford, who was killed in the conflict and who was as fully aware as Owen of the physical horrors

[1] Rex Warner, 'The Tourist looks at Spain' (*New Writing*, 1937, Vol. 4).   [2] *New Writing*, 1939, Vol. 2.

and pain war entailed, who wrote that the greatest fear is
'Flesh still is weak', at the same time embodied in his
poetry the sense that here is the one chance – not for himself as an individual, but for the human race. And it is not
the easy optimism of what up to now Day Lewis had been
writing. The poet is really up against death, and his poetry
embodies the immediacy of war, the immediacy of loss –
in one slight lyric on his march to Huesca he can still write
to his beloved

> Heart of the heartless world,
> Dear heart, the thought of you
> Is the pain at my side,
> The shadow that chills my view.[1]

In spite of this, like most of the young writers of his time,
the poet thinks in terms of countries, nations, of the world,
reflecting the sense of struggle as a world-wide issue:

> Not by any introspection
> Can we regain the name of action,
> Whatever dreams may mean to you, they mean sleep.
> Black over Europe falls the night,
> The darkness of our long retreat,
> And winter closes with a silent grip.[2]

Even in writers who do not deal consciously with war, in
Eliot for instance, there is the constant pointer to the
world being wholly foul. But to these younger writers, the
cause did not lie in 'the taking of a toast and tea' so much
as in the necessity for regaining the name of action.
Fascism was training the minds of its young men to think
in military terms, and the spirit of resistance felt that it
'could not stand apart'. It had above all things a purpose.

> It is the aim that is right and the end is freedom.
> In Spain the veil is torn.
> In Spain is Europe. England also is in Spain.[3]

[1], [2] *New Writing*, 1937. Vol. 4.
[3] 'A Tourist looks at Spain' (*New Writing*, 1937, Vol. 4).

It seemed the single answer to the question of many ills.

To many poets, as Day Lewis's poems on 'The Volunteer' and 'The Nabara' show, to support the Spanish Republican party was an act of patriotism. Warner wrote in 'A Tourist looks at Spain':

> Near Bilbao are buried the vanguard of our army.
> It is us too they defended who defended Madrid.

But this purpose meant to Cornford and the other fighters that

> We must learn to mock at what makes readers wince.

The pity of war will not be found among these poets – among objective observers like Spender and Read – perhaps. But those who fought were poets who 'have no time to stand and stare'. Their verse lacks any approach to the sentimental, is almost lacking in emotion – we might say they were soldiers before they were poets. Without any of the usual patriotic sentiments, without exploiting the usual flag-waving heroics of a just and righteous war, they made a clear statement of their intention in entering the darkness and winter of Europe. Ewart Milne's 'Sierran Vigil' captures something of the Spanish atmosphere, and its laziness seems to invade the sentiments; they are less rousing than stoic:

> Where the lazy wall is down
> Where the lemon leaf is poisoned
> Where the road is holed: where gloom of
> cloud and sky is blessing: we
>> Speaking no good word for war
>> for heroics, for the kingly dust,
>> exalting not the self-evident murder,
>> turn: not assuming hope: turn, offering hands.[1]

It is very much to the point that the three poems of

[1] *New Writing*, 1939, Vol. 2.

Cornford that appeared in 'New Writing' were prefaced by a translation from the Anglo-Saxon:

> Mind shall be harder
> Heart the keener
> Mood the more
>   As our might lessens.

Not that there weren't plenty at home who were doing the flag-waving for them. 'The Nabara' and 'Spain' were no doubt meant to impress the age with its own events. The former especially with its reminiscences of the Armada and Sir Richard Grenville was a call to the stirring heroism of war.

It is doubtful whether writers inquired very deeply into what they were fighting for in terms of Spanish politics – and the fact is significant. The cause gradually became less important than the enemy, for Fascism was a clear-cut enemy, and remained so even when Communism had ceased to appear a clear-cut ally. Any idea about freedom, equality, and brotherhood could suffer disillusionment – but Fascism was inherently pernicious. Spender wrote in his impressions of Germany at the outbreak of war: 'However bad I was, Fascism was worse; by being anti-Fascist I created a rightness for myself besides which personal guilt seemed unimportant.'[1] Orwell in *Homage to Catalonia* tells us that he had not at first thought very much about the political situation before he went to Spain, that came after he had had experience of the many factions that made up the Republic. But, he adds, the one thing that held them together was hatred of a common enemy.

In Spender's verse-drama *Trial of a Judge*, we have a vivid picture of Fascism as the big black villain, in comparison with which Communism is inoffensive, a lamb to the slaughter, more sinned against than sinning. In *New Writing* 1939, Goronwy Rees tells us that the concrete

[1] *World within World* (1951).

political situation of the play allows the characters to exist
as political beings, the Judge symbolising 'the dilemma of
the middle class'. In 1939 the middle class might have
recognised this dilemma of theirs in the Judge, but read
nowadays it is as clear as daylight which side the poet
means us to come down on. There is no doubt which is
black and which is white. Petra's brother is the embodi-
ment of all those who were incited by righteous indigna-
tion to go out and fight in the Spanish Civil War:

> To cross that frontier all I need declare
> Is I have nothing and I give my life
> To those with nothing but their lives.

In a way, the acquiring of a scapegoat was not only a
direct reflection on one political ideology of the age, it not
only reflected the antagonism Fascism was arousing in
non-Fascist countries, but at the same time it was an
escape from thinking that

> It is the world that is wholly foul.

While there was a definite evil to fight against, the men
who were fighting it could not be so bad. They could
even be heroes. For where Eliot had seen man as spiritually sterile, a new aspect was being presented to the 1930s
– to be developed during the Second World War – his
propensity for utter inhuman cruelty. Spender's Judge
declares:

> Since once in my country
> Such a murder is done, and there are eleven million
> Who will applaud the doers, we approach
> Smoking fields of chaos where
> The integral mind melts in collected
> Panic and cruelty.

An age of belittlement, of Shaw and Lytton Strachey and
Huxley, and of a war in which man's personal suffering
was shown up, of Owen and Read and Sassoon, was

degenerating into an age of men whose whole purpose seemed to be to inflict that suffering. It had of necessity to produce its heroes to steal fire from the tyrannical gods. In *The Ascent of F.6*, Auden makes Mr. A. say of the climbers

> But these are prepared to risk their lives in action
> In which the peril is their only satisfaction.
> They have not asked us to alter our lives
> Or to eat less meat or to be more kind to our wives.

As time went on, the Spanish Civil War became not only a clearance of the past and present, but a warning of the future. There was not only disillusionment, as Day Lewis wrote in 'Regency Houses':[1]

> We who in younger days,
> Hoping too much, tried on
> The habit of perfection,
> Have learnt how it betrays
> Our shrinking flesh.

But in the same volume there are several poems, notably 'Newsreel' and 'Bombers' where we are shown the definite evils of war. The poet appeals in the latter, in a way which is typical of him, to basic human feeling on an everyday level:

> Choose between your child and this fatal embryo.

'Newsreel' offers a dig at man's indifference, with an increasing awareness of what war is going to mean to us, even if we are not yet directly involved.

The effect that involvement in actual warfare had on the 1930 writers can be seen if we contrast two plays, both by Auden and Isherwood, *The Ascent of F.6* (1936) and *On the Frontier* (1938). The theme of the age – struggle and achievement and conflict, allegorised in the first in the attempt to conquer a mountain, becomes realised in the

[1] *Overtures to Death* (1938).

second in the war between two states. One mirrors merely an outlook of the age, the other its actual events. Both reflect different stages of the poets' experience. The former lacks the sense of universal calamity embodied in the second. Ransom's tragedy is personal, but that of Eric and Anna seeking 'the good place':

> Where the air is not filled with screams of hatred
> Nor words of great and good men twisted
> To flatter conceit and justify murder.[1]

is one of any young couple caught up in war, a theme to be exploited over and over again during the Second World War.

It is perhaps a trait generally of a century of mass production to regard man as a collective species, but the nature of mass warfare would tend to support this outlook. Once it might have been possible to differentiate between the soldier and the rest of the population, but now there is a sense of man's total involvement as a race. It is why Eric in *On the Frontier* 'could not stand apart'. The sense of man's responsibility was united with the sense of universal suffering that was to come, the conviction that mankind generally was to endure torment – not just the British Army or (in the Spanish War) the idealist who enlisted in the International Brigade. *On the Frontier* belongs to 1938, a year before the Second World War broke out, but the scene was not only set for the fight, destruction was already under way.

> We cannot choose our world,
> Our time, our class. None are innocent, none.
> Causes of violence lie so deep in all our lives
> It touches every act.
> Certain it is for all we do
> We shall pay dearly.[2]

[1] *On the Frontier*, Act 2, Scene 1.
[2] Act 3, Scene 3.

In spite of poems like 'The Nabara', the state of mind of English poets was growing more and more pessimistic. Poems by Auden, Spender and Brecht (in translation) discussed the new problem of exiles and refugees (e.g. 'In Memoriam Ernst Toller', 'Refugee Blues', 'Exiles', 'The Prisoners'). The advance of the tide could be heard even above the Spanish conflict. In 1939 Bernard Gutteridge clinched the connection with his 'Spanish Earth', in which he showed the movement of war from Spain to England:

> Now we can walk into the picture easily
> To be the unknown hero and the death;
> We who have watched these things as stunts
> And held our startled breath.[1]

There is a general awareness, in a large body of poetry produced between 1936 and 1939, of the coming disaster. The Spanish affair was more than an internal squabble in a state of southern Europe. A new element had infiltrated the artist's outlook, a living death had seeped into the pores of life. As Roy Fuller saw it in 1937:

> The rapid death from ordnance
> And the slow from gas, the fascist whip, the nervous
> Horror of workless rotting at home, these are
> Our age, our dreams, and only poetry.[2]

Let us turn from the general comments that war elicited to the many poems that were written on single events during the Spanish conflict by poets who were savouring an experience, where the Spanish landscape and way of life was still a colourful manifesto of age-long traditions. In the field of the novel a writer like Hemingay in *For Whom the Bell Tolls* was combining a support for one side and a sympathetic insight into the mind of a modern American,

[1] *New Writing*, 1939, Vol. 3.
[2] *New Writing*, 1937, Vol. 3.

with a feeling for those traditions and for a people who were steeped in them. Apart from the many Spanish poems that were translated into English at this time, some English poets attempted to write with an eye on Spain alone rather than on Spain in relation to the rest of the world. Let us take Spender as an example.

Especially in this poet, who liked savouring an experience, who could be found sitting on the cliff summit of Port Bou feeling the surge of events and the progress of life around him without the necessity for any sense of purpose to make the scene precious, especially in his work do we find something outside the immediate urges and horrors and claims of the age. The Spanish conflict had a poetic value, possibly because it was remote enough not to touch the poet too nearly except on an intellectual level, and because it could be viewed objectively as a mighty event in the scheme of things, and because it was full of isolated situations that lend themselves to the imagination. The young boy 'lying dead under the olive trees' for instance, or the two armies waiting in between periods of attack:

> When the machines are stilled, a common suffering
> Whitens the air with breath and makes both one
> As though these enemies slept in each other's arms[1]

or the death of a Spanish poet, or the two comrades who are associated with the stopwatch and ordnance map presumably in one of those tiny personal missions that Hemingway described in *For Whom the Bell Tolls*. The war, compared with the world conflict that was to follow, was leisurely enough in parts to provide incidents rather than mass movements or mass destruction.

Spender's sensitivity allows him to sympathise with the fighters whose fate he did not share, and there is at times a similarity between his and Owen's work. But because of

[1] 'Two Armies' (*The Still Centre*, 1939).

D

this perhaps, the two are even more distinguishable in their attitude to war as recreated in their verse, and the wars themselves are differentiated. Even when he uses phrases from Owen, there is a lack of emotional impetus behind his peculiar sensitivity. Pity, anger, hatred, bitterness, pain, are absent in the following verse which is one of the pieces nearest to Owen and at the same time farthest from him:

> Finally they cease to hate: for although hate
> Bursts from the air and whips the earth with hail
> Or shoots it up in fountains to marvel at
> And although hundreds fall who can connect
> The inexhaustible anger of the guns
> With the dumb patience of those tormented animals?[1]

Spender believed in communicating experience, but it is less a dramatic communication than the lyricism of a passing scene. The contrasts that war elicits are present in his verse, but they are not used sharply. That favourite theme of beauty versus ugliness, of the living versus the dead, or pity versus brutality, has its place in Spender, but only because both sides exist to make up one whole element, not because one shows up the other.

Day Lewis mentioned in *A Hope for Poetry* that 'Spender is unlike most of his contemporaries in that he relies for poetic effect considerably on the associational value of his words'. Spender himself tells us in his autobiography that while at Oxford he read Shakespeare, the Elizabethans, the Romantics, the Moderns – and little else. The poetry he produced during the Spanish conflict is the sort we might expect from him in his position of observer. We are always being reminded of the movement of time against the rigid present, of space and eternity outside us in which death has a different meaning. The continual imagery of moon, bones, whiteness, space, and

---

[1] 'Two Armies' (*The Still Centre*, 1939).

time, creates a resemblance to Yeats in its remote loveli-
ness and a tendency to widen the subject on a philosophic
plane:

> And the watch flew off his wrist
> Like a moon struck from the earth
> Marking a blank time that stares
> On the tides of change beneath.[1]

How does a poet like Spender move between the armoured
tank and the ivory tower in a way which he considered it
essential for a poet to do and which is consonant with this
period? First of all we gain a sense from his work of
continual destruction and change, of 'the revolving and
dissolving world'. Nothing is fixed, nothing can be
gauged.

> He saw the flagship at the quay,
> His mother's care, his father's kiss,
> The white accompaniment of spray,
> Lead to the bullet and to this.
> Flesh, bone, muscle, eyes
> Built in their noble tower of lies,
> Scattered on the icy breeze
> Him their false promises betrayed.[2]

Then there is the feeling common in the period that we
must get back to more human sentiments. Love is emphasised in Spender, Auden, and Day Lewis. The latter in *A
Hope for Poetry* gave an explanation of why poets of the
time started from love, namely because it was necessary to
re-establish brotherhood before poetic contact could be
made. In both *Trial of a Judge* and *On the Frontier* it is
seen as the one thing that conquers, even against the
terrors and political ideologies of the period.

Then again, as we have noted before, a more realistic
display of conflict entered poetry once bloodshed had

[1] 'A Stopwatch and an Ordnance Map' (*The Still Centre*).
[2] 'The Coward'.

actually begun in Europe. In Spender there is an extravagant display of it in *Trial of a Judge* where the Fascists describe Petra's shooting:

> We dragged him screaming
> Out of the straw bed by the heels.
> I shot him, stripped. Then we stamped on him
> And kicked his face in.

But in the poems on the Spanish Civil War, Spender expresses much of the violence of the age indirectly through the imagery. The loved one he describes as hidden

> In sunbright peninsulas of the sword:
> Torn like leaves through Europe is the peace
> That through us flowed.[1]

European calamity and personal are merged as the age's rupture is expressed in the form of one individual's absence from another. *World Within World* could apply to Spender's style as well as his life.

His is a completely different method from that of a poet like MacNeice who in his *Autumn Journal* (1938) has several passages on Spain and on England facing an impending crisis. We could very well read this as an interesting documentary of the time; its purpose is to tell us what is happening at one particular moment in one particular place. This insularity, while at the same time being able to express aptly and wittily the ordinary thoughts of an educated man of the period, is MacNeice's peculiar gift.

> You can't step in the same river twice so there can't be
> Ghosts: thank God that rivers always flow.

Such sentiments might have been the daily self-encouragement of any ordinary thinker just before the outbreak of war, the attempt to convince oneself that another war can't

[1] 'The Room above the Square'.

possibly take place. Yet at the same time we learn directly from MacNeice that 'The New Year comes with bombs'.

In Spender we are more likely to find the poignancy of the period's tragedy:

> And although there is gold in the corn and gaiety
> In a girl's eyes or sliding along the stream,
> Everything is without a meaning.[1]

[1] *Trial of a Judge.*

CHAPTER FOUR

Auden and Campbell

BEFORE leaving the Spanish Civil War we should perhaps remember that there was the other side to the question, many of whose supporters viewed the fight as a stand
for Catholicism and traditional values. They found their
voice in English poetry in Roy Campbell. He was a poet
brought up in South Africa with results comparable to
those of Kipling's Mowgli being brought up by wolves.
The latter never forgot that he belonged to the human
race, though he found it difficult to return to it. The
former never forgot that he was an Englishman, though
he could never return wholeheartedly to English institu-
tions and ways of thinking. A Catholic himself, he fought
on the Franco side of the Spanish conflict, and wrote from
direct military experience of events (unlike some of the
English intellectuals who, like Auden, merely looked in
and looked out again). He was from the beginning aware
that his poetry was running against the grain of contemporary English writing.

We have in Stephen Spender's autobiography, a
picture of W. H. Auden at Oxford, judging, encouraging,
changing, and directing the work of his contemporaries,
in an attempt to set up a new school of poets to express the
new age. *Flowering Rifle* which was Campbell's 'epic' on
the Spanish Civil War, published in 1939, pictures

> the fat snuggery of Auden, Spender,
> And others of the self-same breed and gender,
> Who hold by guile the fort of English letters . . .

Between 1929 and 1939, Auden had planned, made, and

succeeded in his attack on the fort of English letters. Campbell might, as his enemy in politics, style, and temperament, accuse him of employing guile, but he has all the same to admit that the fort is his. And it is when we measure Campbell against Auden and his new school of poetry, that we see how the former possessed those very qualities that were ruled out in the England of the between-war years. From his position outside the fat snuggery Campbell sees

> Some self-aborted pedants stray forlorn
> And pity those who venture to be born –
> Born, if they knew it, in the Morning's pride
> When never Death was sweeter to deride
> Nor Life so fresh and fiery for the ride.

People living in England after the First World War and the disillusioning years of peace that followed it, were not accustomed to thinking of the world as young. The thoughts that occupied Prufrock were the signs of advancing age. In his 'Georgiad' Campbell mocks at one who was

> Still in his tender disillusion sore
> Because, ten years ago, there was a war.

This exuberance is typical of Campbell. Edith Sitwell later called him a 'poetic tornado', and some of the energy of the wild powerful open-air life he was brought up to, as he relates in his autobiography, *Light on a Dark Horse*, emerges both in his style and his attitude to experience. As a retort to the 'contemporary' poetry that saw society in terms of sickness, Campbell uses satire to make those who belittle mankind seem small:

> For life and history are heroic things
> . . . with the sagas and the myths they'll run
> Rejoicing with the seasons and the sun.

A tonic for weariness, disillusionment, boredom, and cynicism, Campbell stands out among the poets of his time, and knows it:

As for myself I glory in my crime –
Of English poets first in all my time
To sock the bleary monster in my rhyme.

He is quite determined that his life will end with a bang,
not with a whimper. Not even the horrors of the Second
World War could depress his ebullience or prevent him
loving

the hard and stony track
Where humour flashes from the flint.[1]

Campbell's intense faith in life and in himself, in man
generally being able to rise above his situation, places him,
as I have said before, outside a period whose poets were
desperately desirous of capturing the contemporary
malaise. This is to assume that the hallmark of the age lies
in the city. Campbell belongs neither to the age of cities
nor the age of anxiety.

Although Campbell's is a peculiarly personal reply to
challenge, his poetry does, it seems to me, bring out a
quality which existed in the Spanish Civil War and which
distances it from that which went before and that which
was to come after. In spite of the use made of Spain as a
training-ground for Mussolini's planes and the coming
Communo-Fascist conflict, some of the causes that were
being fought for were old as well as new. Spain was probably the least European of all the European countries, and
much of the fighting permitted a certain kind of heroics
that finds better voice in Campbell than in Auden's
picture of an age where

bravery is now
Not in the dying breath
But resisting the temptations
To skyline operations.

When we turn to Auden, we find a poet who from the
very beginning, according to Spender, ruled that a good

[1] 'Monologue' (*Collected Poems*).

poem should be 'symptomatic' and show 'contemporary sensibility'. The poet should himself be clinical and detached, an 'ordinary man', 'dressed like a bank clerk'. From these statements we should expect objective description of war and world events because these are symptomatic of the age's interest. Spender has told us in his autobiography that Auden never had a Communist phase – ' "A Communist to Others" is an exercise in entering into a point of view not his own.' And again Spender has described 'Spain' as 'the best poetic statement in English of the Republican case'.

It is part of Auden's gift to allow himself to be deeply enough involved in the thought of his age to capture its partisan mode of thinking and yet remain uncommitted to what he writes. It is not surprising that Campbell with his personal enthusiasm (which approaches more nearly to Day Lewis's attitude than to that of any other poet of the Auden group), should have taken exception to the dry, probing quality of Auden's verse, and have used the Spanish issue to attack a poetic manner which was so opposed to his own.

Campbell affects something of the 'grand' style, and when it comes to war in *Flowering Rifle* we are among a welter of flying bullets, ravages, and lurid ferocities. It is from Campbell that we can expect an insight into the battle area of Spain, and he is a poet who rarely spares the detail. He pursues the usual propagandist war technique of lauding his own side and castigating his opponents. Possibly due to his strongly individualist temperament whatever Campbell chooses to deal with, whether it be the sorrows of war or the more humorous side of life, what comes over to us is his joy and his enthusiasm —

Life and I, with time to spare . . .

No English 1930 poet who took politics and the world situation seriously or even his position as a 'contemporary' poet, could have made such a remark. Campbell was inclined to take events and politics as they came – during the Spanish Civil War he was pro-Fascist, during the Second World War he was pro-British – he acted upon his own experience of how a country flourishes under various kinds of government. He lived in Spain for some time before the war and could boast of being one who had

> Lived beneath the two régimes
> And have not dreamed the Leftie Teacher's dreams.

The circumstances of the century have sided with the Leftie teacher and against Campbell. Even had his talent been comparable with Auden's, the Second World War, reiterating the tragedy of the Great War would have prevented him from being the man concurring with the moment. In standing slightly aloof from the Spanish conflict Auden was possibly closer to the general temper of the century.

In other ways Auden is close to the general temper of the century, in particular in presenting us with what is no longer conventional war poetry, in reflecting an age in which war has come to mean something more than just battles and trench or hand-to-hand fighting – from 'The Secret Agent' in which we see the underhand consequences of enmity exemplified in the spy system, to 'The Shield of Achilles' in which we have the usual everyday signs that a state of war exists, the shooting of prisoners at dawn, the line up of an army, looking, acting, and thinking in the manner war imposes upon it —

> A million eyes, a million boots in line,
> Without expression waiting for a sign.

Auden's 'war' poetry, speaking impersonally during the Spanish conflict, and increasing in irony and astringency during and after the Second World War, has tried to reflect the problems and tragedy of the age. In an early poem, 'Which side am I supposed to be on?', there is something trivial and futile in the demands we make upon life:

> Are you in training?
> Are you taking care of yourself? are you sure of passing
> The endurance test?

A later work, 'In Time of War', not only shows us the meanness of our present way of life, but goes further, and shows us the smallness of man's nature:

> The groping searchlights suddenly reveal
> The little natures that will make us cry.

All of man's neuroses come out in this century – how he

> spoke approvingly of Law and Order,
> And hated life with all his soul

> And gathered into crowds and was alone.

The same poem gives us the modern rendering of the unknown soldier theme, only without the conventional eulogy:

> He will not be introduced
> When this campaign is tidied into books:
> No vital knowledge perished in his skull;
> His jokes were stale; like wartime, he was dull;
> His name is lost forever like his looks.

It is the cruel answer to a cruel age. We are not raised spiritually by this man's death because he himself

> neither knew nor chose the Good.

The loss of the ideal against which to measure reality emerges time and time again in Auden's work. In connection with our theme of war we find it most clearly stated in a late poem, 'The Shield of Achilles', where the horrifying scenes that Thetis sees portrayed in the shield are set against the ideals we have of the past that belong to a world of art, and at the same time, the mother who desires that the world should be idealised in her son's shield is contrasted with Achilles, the son as he really is, even in his own time no more than a man-slayer.

Campbell, in his attack on the poets of 'the other side' viewed them as contributing in their social criticism to the disease of the times – disillusionment. His contempt for an age that makes gods

> Of Economics, Science, Gold, and Sex.

makes him turn instead with renewed faith to a country that

> repudiates the breed that barters
> And owns the sway of heroes, saints, and martyrs.

What he left out of consideration was the fact that Auden and the '30s poets generally were writing from within the area that Campbell condemns and whatever the manner of presentation, were deeply committed to a particular end. Louis MacNeice tells us that whereas Eliot had sat back and observed,

> The whole poetry, on the other hand, of Auden, Spender, and Day Lewis implies that they have desires and hatreds of their own and, further, that they think some things OUGHT to be desired and others hated.[1]

When Campbell hurled his accusation at these poets, that they were adding to the perversion of life, he was disregarding the role they set themselves in all good faith as physicians, attempting to make a diagnosis before it was too late. We must remember Spender's criticism of *Flowering Rifle*. He can hardly contain himself in his determination that the last word shall be a defence of his own beliefs: 'Mr. Campbell indignantly repudiates the accusation that he is a Romantic. He is quite right, for the Romantics were distinguished by their disinterested passion for truth, equalled only by their love of freedom and justice.'[2]

[1] *Modern Poetry* (1938).   [2] *New Statesman*, March 11th, 1939.

CHAPTER FIVE

1939
The Older Generation of Poets

WHEN the dreams of Utopia had been finally dissolved with the failure of the Spanish Civil War, the world awoke to the coming horrors. Because of the nature of the Second World War, it was not just the young men or the fighters who sampled the onrush of battle. Where, in the First World War, there had been a distinct difference between being at the front and returning home on leave, it might during the Second World War have been more of a disadvantage to return to a bombarded London than to remain on duty in a fairly quiet outpost. It meant that war could be experienced by all generations, whether fit for active service or not, and it also meant that poets both male and female and of widely varying age and life were caught up in it.

It might well be expected that a poet who lived through both wars would look at the second one with different eyes from the young men who were sampling fighting for the first time. To consider the differences and similarities there are between the work of dissimilar generations, I shall divide the writers into three groups, the older generation, many of whom had fought during the First World War – the middle generation born at the opening of the century, who had grown up during the First World War, and many of whom had formed the nucleus of Spanish Civil War supporters – and finally the younger generation who usually write from their positions on the battlefield.

The older generation, including men like Blunden, Read, Church, and Graves, form a rather miscellaneous group. For although years of war may draw men together if not in a single cause at least through common experience, years of peace are likely to divide them, sending each along his separate path. And they will bring to the mere observation of a second war twenty years later, not simply the memories they might share of the previous fight, but at the same time all those years of separation that lie between. In spite of this the Second World War seems to have drawn from them thoughts and feelings that distinguish them as a group.

Herbert Read is perhaps the poet who most clearly moved in a straight line from the First to the Second World War, partly because the years between he spent with an eye on the political situation after his personal experience of European conflict, and hence reflected part of the movement of history. He was caught up in the intellectual thought of his age, mirroring its trials and needs, its search for an answer in a form of Communism, and its subsequent disillusionment.

During the Second World War he deliberately looks back and has a continual sense of the failure of the years between the wars. In the Preface to his autobiography he wrote: 'These pages will make sufficiently clear that I consider the no-man's years between the wars as largely futile, spent unprofitably by me and all my kind.'[1]

'To a Conscript of 1940' sums up the disillusionment of those people who lived through the first war and hoped for great things from it. The Second World War has given the final blow to a structure that was already crumbling in the years of hardship that followed 1918.

> We think we gave in vain. The world was not renewed.
> There was hope in the homestead and anger in the streets
> But the old world was restored and we returned

[1] *Annals of Innocence and Experience.*

To the dreary field and workshop, and the immemorial
    feud
Of rich and poor.[1]

Now there is retribution, with the young paying for the
faults of their fathers.

Like many of the older generation, Read gives the impression of puzzlement that this has happened before, and
now it is happening again. The older poets are never tired
of saying in one way or another – 'This is not the first
time !' From this arises a sense of history, a feeling for the
age in its place among all other ages, that perhaps only
older people can really grasp. In 'The Contrary Experience', Read sees history repeating itself:

> Libya, Egypt, Hellas,
> the same tide ebbing, the same gull crying.[2]

Yet he realises that war itself is changed,

> the crusade heart outshatter'd.[3]

The answer is one we shall find in the other writers of this
group, to go on in spite of everything, and knowing the
hopelessness of it —

> To fight without hope is to fight with grace,
> The self reconstructed, the false heart repaired.[4]

To reach this point the poet has been through despair at
the condition of man. The intellectual agnosticism that
opened the century meant that our period is one that relies
on a belief in man rather than God. Now that this disaster
has struck, only those with faith in God 'can wait patiently
for the end'.

[1, 2] *A World within a War*.
[3] 'War and Peace' (*A World within a War*).
[4] 'To a Conscript of 1940' (*A World within a War*).

It is from the older generation that we might look for a decrial of all the flagwaving that poets did at the opening of the First World War. Read tells us that he has learnt what heroism really is, the reality and not the ideal, there are no illusions left now. He has also learnt what sacrifice means and he writes to advise the young. His whole attitude is that of the onlooker, the man who knows because he has had experience of it. He represents that generation that had to accustom itself once again to a terror that it had already fought one war to end. Yet, having one foot in the past, it also looks forward to the next phase of history in the future.

> The root deep in the dark soil of the past
> But deeper in the unform'd future
> Is folded the flower.[1]

In 'A World within a War', the poet retires to a secret world and preaches inward peace, going back to the way in which friars and martyrs found grace, forgiving and nulling pain. Even as early as 'Kneeshaw goes to war' the poet sought to prove how important is the individual soul and its response to life in general. His concluding thoughts on the First World War are to be found in *The End of a War* (1933) in which he touches on the meaning of life and God's part, through three dramatic monologues. There, one alternative conclusion he came to was that this is the world's last tragic act. The Second World War proved that this was not so, so much so that in his autobiography Read sees the crisis as one of a young world breaking through its parent bondage. But it is not until *A World within a War* (1944) that we feel that he is finding a personal re-assurance. There is hope in the future if not joy, and a search for the healing of those wounds opened by the disillusionment of 1914–18.

Edmund Blunden was another poet who fought in and

---

[1] Dunkirk 'Ode' (*A World within a War*).

wrote on the First World War, much more in fact than on the Second. In 'War's People' he told us

> We went, returned,
> But came with that far country learned.[1]

The impression left by the First World War was so distinct that it became part of man's consciousness. Like those of other poets, his memories in his early poems were full of pity and horror, of the hardness of death because death was never desired, a death full of harsh detail, lacking all graciousness —

> Worley with a tot of rum
> And shouting in his face could not restore him.[2]

The pastoral nature of his early poetry is combined with this strong realism —

> the lean green flies upon the red flesh madding[3]

to indicate the

> weary hate of foul and endless war.

Like the rest of his generation, Blunden was bitter about the 'vicarious heroes', and did not hesitate to attack where attack was needed. His preoccupation with the subject can be seen in the number of times he recalled the First World War during the peace years.

But the Second World War poetry is like an *Oedipus at Colonus* following an *Oedipus Rex*. The volume entitled *After the Bombing* has very little reference to actual warfare and death – it shows mainly the gradual growth of peace and how nature is never deterred by man's upheavals.

> That brown patch in the wood is where the last bomb
>   shattered

[1] *Poems 1914–30.*
[2] 'Pillbox' (*Undertones of War*).
[3] 'Third Ypres' (*Undertones of War*).

E

> And next year's bluebells wait to show how much it
> mattered.[1]

Compared with the photographic accounts of life in the
trenches in 1914–18 his description of bombs during the
Second World War in 'When the Statue Fell', is light,
romantic, almost flippant:

> Heard a new voice, of thunder-throated things
> Behind the hills, and hideous travellings
> Of airy devils; into roof and room
> These raced their way and ruptured into smoke,
> And here and there and everywhere outbroke
> The mad plague murderous.[2]

The most piteous poem is 'For the Fallen' and even there
the note is one of pathos rather than bitterness. That same
bitterness of the First World War was replaced by the
realisation that this war is different from others, that men
chose to enter it of their own free will knowing exactly
what it means:

> So you have chosen, saying little, knowing
> That surface paths are counted easier going,
> That other wars make quicker, gaudier showing.[3]

Turning to 'Inter Arma' we find a quiet optimism about
what man desires, and therefore hope for the future:

> Being asked to conceive that the fortune of war now raging
> In forms of blazing metal and desperate valour
> Will settle the question of life worth living or not
> For a century hence, I could only doubt the relevance
> Of such slant argument.

> Through transient stress, young love and grace return.
> What war decides, though slow we are to learn,
> Is war's concern.[4]

[1] 'Southern England in 1944) (*After the Bombing*).
[2] *After the Bombing*.
[3] 'The Boy on Leave' (*Shells by a Stream*).
[4] *After the Bombing*.

Richard Church, by contrast with Blunden is a poet who has written practically nothing on the First World War but a great deal on the Second. He writes usually from the standpoint of the small individual who turns to his gardening for security in this world tornado. At the same time he is aware of old age, of belonging more entirely to a previous war, of being an onlooker. He refers to 'your generation' as knowing

> The worst that can befall the race of man[1]

and speaks of himself as one of

> The scannel-piped scareboys on the old battlefield.[2]

'The Wartime Singers' at the same time gives us a picture of the young generation refusing to listen to the old, and eliciting from them a certain admiration for their

> strange, hard music, compounded on different laws.

The fact that he has written hardly anything on the First World War does not mean that he was not perfectly aware of its horrors, or that he did not have the same memories of the ogre. He later wrote of how

> Twenty years ago
> My generation learned
> To be afraid of mud.
> We watched its vileness grow,
> Deeper and deeper churned
> From earth, spirit, and blood[3]

But with the Second World War the poet really comes into his own. He shows an awareness similar to Read's of events in their place in history. The position is different in that Church speaks from the viewpoint of a religious man and draws most of his examples from the Bible. What is still

---

[1] 'Riding up the Hill' (*The Solitary Man*).
[2] 'The Wartime Singers' (*Twelve Noon*).
[3] 'Mud' (*Twelve Noon*).

continuing through the centuries is man's humanity and its burden of original sin:

> Our art and science
> No longer feature hell and paradise.
> But still the ancient longing and regret
> Govern our actions; still the old defiance.[1]

Church not only takes up a religious attitude towards the war, seeing the solution as lying in God's hands, but he distils certain values from it for the benefit of the people enduring at home. As well as speaking for a certain public, faith and generation, Church is consciously aware of his age in terms of history. He sees the insecurity of his particular period and at the same time its disgrace.

> We shall not be forgotten; we shall be
> Like Ozymandias, self-named King of Kings,
> A monument to man's fatuity
> When an ironic god first gave him wings.[2]

Like Read, Richard Church is a reflective poet. His task is to ponder the life of today rather than give us an exact picture of it. His poetry in consequence goes deeply into causes and reasons, analyses the 'spirit of the age', sees how man has lost his sense of wonder in

> A world self-conscious even in its fear,
> Scorning its few surviving superstitions,
> Condemning love as a romantic fraud.[1]

Like Read and Blunden, Church has hope for the future. The emphasis of his *Twentieth Century Psalter* is on joy and love – the title itself indicates its religious character. The very horrors of war make the poet feel that at least we have known the worst. He himself has

> Groped near the ground for the moisture of faith.

and he finds that the willow and quince he has planted as

1, 2, 3 *Twentieth Century Psalter.*

a sign of sorrow and bitterness have flowered – that the desert can blossom like the rose. War makes us aware of the transient nature of things, but the poet looks ahead and sees that when war and its desecration have passed we will find that they have lent some meaning to life it would otherwise have lacked. He expresses it in a popular image of the bomb damage —

> Charred passion, and a broken wall,
> Make ruins that will lean
> With more significance than the unrifled
> Originals now mean.[1]

Robert Graves's first introduction to the public was as a war poet during the 1914–18 conflict. As he himself has stated, the fashion for writing 'war poetry' was such that he had started even before he reached the front. His early volumes *Over the Brazier* and *Fairies and Fusiliers* which gained him some reputation are in tune both with the Georgian love of pasture and peace, and the fashionable war realism. They are possibly more indicative of the time than of Graves's poetic merit, and tend to display a rather coolly objective approach. Later, when he came to select from his early work for the 1926 Collected Edition of his poems he felt, he related later, that he could not conscientiously reprint any of his war poems. They were 'too obviously written in the war-poetry boom'.[2]

The years between the wars, though at first bitten into considerably by the left-over neurosis of war, saw Graves developing his own individual themes and style and taking up much more of a lone-wolf position than most of his contemporaries. He was in any case absent from England for much of the 1930 decade. The Second World War saw him too firmly fixed in his own pursuit of the Muse or the White Goddess whose image came to dominate his poetry,

[1] 'Be Patient' (*The Solitary Man*).
[2] *The Listener*, October 23rd, 1941.

for him to ever return to poetry of mere social significance. Trying in 1941 to answer the question why the Second World War had produced no war poets when the First World War had produced so many, he viewed it as part of a situation that existed in the First World War that no longer existed during the Second. Now that conscription was imposed, poets were no longer needed for the recruiting campaign, and the make-up of the army was different. 'It is no longer,' he states, 'the amateur, desperate, happy-go-lucky, ragtime, lousy army of World War I.'[1] The whole training of the new army is different: 'The sort of soldier who in World War I would naturally have become a "war-poet" now feels a khaki-blanco mist rise between him and the world of his imagination.'

In a Postscript to this article in 1949 Graves speaks of war poetry as a 'higher kind of journalism' for which the need disappeared when highly trained journalists could serve reports to the nation. He thinks the tortuous modern style young poets employed was certainly not suited to this 'higher kind of journalism' and when speaking of John Pudney he designates him simply as a 'verse-reporter'.

It is hardly surprising that Graves whose Muse was in *loco religionis* did not by this time consider it the task of a 'serious' poet to produce war poetry. And in fact there is only a small body of poetry making up his 1938–45 output. The war no doubt brought certain images to mind but they are used in the development of Graves's individual themes. There is the mention of a dawn bombardment, and in 'Lucia at birth' there is the picture of the moon rising in a world of burning corn and feuding heraldic beasts, but this is the situation from time immemorial, and Graves ends by calling upon the moon

Nothing will change them, let them not change you.

A very typical poem 'Spoils', in a later volume, is a

[1] *The Listener*, October 23rd, 1941

simple two-verse apposition of the spoils of war and the spoils of love. When Graves speaks of the

> lesser gleanings of the battle-field –
> Coins, watches, wedding rings, gold teeth and such

he is displaying the same analytical detachment that he set out with in the First World War. But his preoccupation now is with something different. The metaphysics of feeling emerge in the comparison between the disposable nature of the spoils of war – either to decorate a home, or to sell for cash – and the slavery of the individual soul to the relics of love that can never be disposed of but are more likely in their turn to consume.

So with the exception of Graves who seems to stand outside the question, most of this older generation of poets think along similar lines, whatever their basic differences. All of them view the war in a way similar to E. M. Forster's description in *Howards End* of Beethoven's Fifth Symphony – the goblins are there walking from one end of the world to the other, but always the light and the romance and chivalry floods back – yet the memory of the goblin predominates. After all, they had lived long enough to see that goblin come and go – and come back again. Not that the Second World War was a repetition of the Passchendaele trenches, but that this generation of poets retains the memory of the First World War, resulting on occasion among lesser poets in a kind of throwback. So in Herbert Palmer there is the First World War echo that this race of Huns needs putting down. In a poet like Edward Shanks there is a return to the glory of England and her heroes' theme.

The great strength of this generation lies in their awareness of the past in the present. Their great weakness lies in their inability to grasp the distinctive flavour of the present, because they are not as completely part of it as a younger generation is likely to be.

CHAPTER SIX

1939
The Middle Generation of Poets

As representative of the middle generation of poets, let us look at the group that flourished in the '30s – Spender, Day Lewis, Auden, Lehmann, and MacNeice. It is just as difficult to see the similarities between them as poets as between the older writers. But listened to as a group, although they speak with different voices, what we hear might well turn out to be the same thing in the end.

What strikes us first and foremost is that these poets who took the lead in verbally revolutionising the world in the 1930s, are at a loss once Europe is at war, to find any clear clarion call that can be blown. To begin with, war had scattered them to settle their own accounts in the disrupted universe – Auden and Isherwood to America, Spender in the fire service, and Day Lewis in the home guard. All of them had made their mark in the poetic world and no longer needed each other from a professional point of view. But their work gives the impression that war has interrupted something. Day Lewis chafes at the bit when asked 'Where are the war poets?' and speaks of poetry now as a necessity for the world rather than a pleasure for the poet. The Second World War did away with the enthusiasm for change and a new dawn breaking that we find in a poem like 'The Magnetic Mountain'. Where the First World War had been the direct inspiration of many writers, this group of poets during the Second World War wanted to get on with the business of writing poetry, and the war was a side issue that not only kept intruding itself upon their notice, but involved duties that kept them from the actual writing (apart, of course, from Auden). Spender, in fact, tells us that he joined the fire service in order to go on being a poet.

As a group, these poets have much in common in not being fighters. Theirs is the home-front background. *Trial of a Judge* and *On the Frontier* had laid their scenes in the middle of continental warfare, but with the outbreak of 1939, it seemed as if surrounding detail was too pressing for the mind to wander into a realm that was not of the poet's immediate experience. Therefore these poets tend to speak on behalf of the men at home, the ordinary civilian who suffered bomb damage and knew only of Tobruk and Dachau and Nanking from the radio.

They are particularly well cut out for this position. As a generation of social satirists they are always aware of the way the world around them looks. In fact the great value of this group of poets lies in their combination of the immediate homely element as the ordinary man might see it, with wider issues. Whereas poets like Owen and Sassoon had been forced by war to take up the position of satirists, these poets were satirists of society to begin with. The war accomplished no change in this direction, it merely turned them into recorders of events and feelings that belong to a special six-year period.

What drains these poets of the revolutionary enthusiasm of their early work is the failure of their ideals. They are continually harking back to their own position in the scheme of events and their pessimism over the world situation is bound up with their disillusionment over those ideals. When John Lehmann writes

> Our peace is only that we see
> Tomorrow may make others well,[1]

he is pre-supposing not only the age's unrest but his own generation's failure to make men well today.

[1] 'The End' (*The Age of the Dragon*, 1951).

Although Auden, after his departure to America, turned to religion, his work does not seem to have become less despairing in consequence. All the poets of this group were aware of the approach of war long before it broke out, partly through their awareness of what was going on on the continent, and Auden's main contribution to this was his play, in collaboration with Isherwood, *On the Frontier* (1938). It had much to say in Shavian fashion about the dictatorships that evolved during the 1930s – in its accent on the man of power and his complete control of mankind. But its central tragic theme is war, war of our time – in the background the song of the soldiers with its echoes of 1914–18 – in the foreground the innocent who are put on opposite sides of the fence, the lovers who are torn apart. A sense of guilt pervades the play that it is not simply the corruption of government that brings this about, but 'the world that is wholly foul'. Eric's speech at the end is moving because it turns to tragedy the very fact that we are of this particular age and time, an age of guilt and sorrow and suffering, present and to come:

> We cannot choose our world,
> Our time, our class. None are innocent, none.
> Causes of violence lie so deep in all our lives
> It touches every act.
> Certain it is for all we do
> We shall pay dearly.

But there is still to be found in this play a belief in the 'good place', even though Eric and Anna are not allowed to find it. It bridges both the idealism of the '30s and the blacker realism of the '40s. Yet the non-romantic note it strikes, while at the same time being an imaginary situation, belongs singularly to the year 1938, the year of the shadow of 1939 —

> And maps can really point to places
> Where life is evil now.[1]

The great danger, Auden is saying, is not really war itself, but what man is becoming – Valerian's speech contains something of Shaw's Undershaft:

> This is probably the last period of human history. The political régimes of the future may have many fancy names, but never again will the common man be allowed to rule his own life or judge for himself. To be an artist or a saint has ceased to be modern . . . yes, for the man of power there can now be but one aim – absolute control of mankind.

The war was the climax and at the same time the eruption of the atmosphere that had been gradually built up in the 1930s. The hope of finding 'the good place' is gone. The poems in *Journey to a War* which just preceded the actual outbreak in September show of how little significance the actual entry of England into the European conflict was as a date-line. The intellectual world was ready for the Second World War as it had never been for any previous war. 'In Time of War' was in the same volume, and in this poem we are told that war has become real, inevitably real, on a far vaster scale than the Spanish conflict.

> Yes, we are going to suffer now; the sky
> Throbs like a feverish forehead; pain is real;
> The groping searchlights suddenly reveal
> The little natures that will make us cry.
>   Who never quite believed they could exist,
>   Not where we were.

Although this generation of poets was capable of anticipating the outbreak of war, it was not immediately capable of accepting it. A poem like this reflects the incredulity; reality has become too real to believe in. Perhaps it was

[1] 'In Time of War' (*Journey to a War*, 1939).

because of their former hopes, not so much of what the
world might become, as of their ability to make their
mark upon it, that when war came it meant personal
failure as well as world chaos:

> The Good Place has not been; our star has warmed to
> birth
> A race of promise that has never proved its worth.[1]

Auden's poetry is full of the sense of betrayal, everything
has been a sham and nothing true. The voyager on his
quest for the good place or the juster life –

> 'discovers nothing; he does not want to arrive.
> The journey is false; the false journey really an illness
> On the false island where the heart cannot act and will not
> suffer.'[1]

Apart from looking back on the failure of the 'pink
decade', this generation of poets recalls less of the past
than the older, understandably so. But they have an
awareness of the future, and of the future's opinion of the
present, of this dark age. As I said earlier, Auden expresses
the sentiment, 'Can any good thing come out of
Nazareth?'

> Can future ages ever escape so far,
> Yet feel derived from everything that happened,
> Even from us, that even this was well?[3]

The bitterness is not against war specifically as in 1914–
18, but against the status to which man's life is reduced
partly as a result of war. There is no longer a clear issue,
a poet can only 'defend the bad against the worse'.

Two of Auden's shorter lyrics, 'Refugee Blues' and
'First September, 1939'[4] record not just war as such, but
war of a particular age. They record attitudes of the

---

[1] 'In Time of War'.   [2] 'The Voyage' (*Journey to a War*).
[3] 'In Time of War' (*Journey to a War*). [4] *Another Time* (1940).

human race as if fossilized in their layer of time. Suffering and indifference in the former are not feelings but states of man. In the latter the shallowness of New York is expressed by its outer aspect, for it is an age when those outer aspects serve the poet singularly well in expressing what the inner man has become:

> Faces along the bar
> Cling to their average day:
> The lights must never go out,
> The music must always play.

The Age of Anxiety does the same job on a larger scale. It sees war's effect on society and as part of that society. The seediness of life is increased by the clinical analysis of a world grown dull with excess. Malin's tale of action, for instance, related ironically in Anglo-Saxon metre, lacks both colour, and the excitement and emotion of the Anglo-Saxon world. There is nothing epic about our way of life – the Leader, the Fourth man at a conference, is not of epic stature, he enters a side door —

> Quick, quiet, unquestionable as death,
> Grief or guilt.

The Lord of this life

> Smiles well, he smells of the future,
> Odourless ages, an ordered world
> Of planned pleasure and passport control.

The world, the poet points out, is in the hands of men like this, a world of smallness and of the unheroic – not deliberately so as in the 1930s, but inevitably now.

The accounts of warfare hold none of the old heroics – men suffer but do not fight, hospital trains move with sensitised freight, men lie bandaged in barns

> Their poor hands in a panic of need
> Groping weakly for a gun-butt or
> A friendly fist.

Here we have pity and terror on a wide scale but not on a grand scale. Auden's *Age and Anxiety* would be heavy-going without the element of astringent criticism it contains. This particular dialogue plumbs the depths of man as a 'new barbarian' bred by civilisation:

> college towns
> Mothered his mind, and many journals
> Backed his beliefs.

War is all of a piece with what civilisation has become: When victory is finally declared,

> behind the festooned
> Conqueror's car there come his heirs, the
> Public hangman, the private wastrel.

There is a great difference in fact between the conception of war of Auden's generation and that of the 1914–18 poets. What lies between is Mr. Eliot's patient, etherized upon a table. To Owen and Sassoon war was horrible in itself, to Auden it is a 'symptom' of a greater horror. That is why war as a subject on its own is rarely touched upon by this generation of poets, why people might well ask 'Where are the war poets?'

The protests against the First World War demanded peace. But Auden makes Rosetta say

> Lies and lethargies police the world
> In its periods of peace. What pain taught
> Is soon forgotten; we celebrate
> What ought to happen as if it were done,
> Are blinded by our boasts.[1]

This generation had seen men of the First World War hoping and being disappointed, and while they do not emphasise those hopes because they had not been old enough to share in them, they are nevertheless aware of

[1] *Age of Anxiety.*

men's inability to reap in peace what they had not sown in war.

But *The Age of Anxiety* was published in 1948 when the war was safely tucked away in its black box, and when it was obvious that peace meant simply a cease-fire in Europe. Its clinical quality might be due to the fact that now the worst was over the poet, like the rest of the world, could adopt a dry ironic note. By contrast, 'New Year Letter', which was produced during the war, is one of Auden's most strikingly personal poems in its expression of feeling. There the world itself is the suffering Prometheus, suffering from its own fault perhaps – but still suffering. The poet voices the fears of his time, the lack of determination, the sense of being lost in the world. The New Year is 1941, and as Auden wrote

> The New Year brings an earth afraid.

Auden captures some of that fine spirit of sadness that occurs in literature just before the peak of battle – the Anglo-Saxon, Henry V before Agincourt, Frodo and Sam in face of the shadow of Sauron, Tolstoy's Prince André – all of them bear the same marks of some common experience in the hour before the darkness closes :

> Only on battlefields, where the dying
> With low voices and not very much to say
> Repair the antique silence the insects broke
> In an architectural passion,
> Can night return to our cooling fibres.

At the same time he is torn by the pity of it, for war is to life what it is to his poetry – an image of something gone wrong, of what man himself is —

> For we are conscripts to our age
> Simply by being born, we wage
> The war we are.

To describe man at this time in terms of war is to describe

him at his most miserable – the sentiment might have
come from a tragic hero. Only the story of this tragedy is
unnecessary to the audience, the stage has become real
life, as MacNeice stated afterwards —

> we walked a stage
> With real thunder off.[1]

The dominant note of Auden's 'New Year Letter' is of a
child crying out in the dark – we have completely lost our
way

> O not ever war can frighten us enough

On occasions Auden's poetry suggests there might be
some road that leads out of the maze, but those occasions
are rare, and it is only a suggestion that one day

> the fever shall have a cure, the true journey an end
> Where hearts meet and are really true.[2]

Auden speaks for an age, not like Eliot looking on, nor
like Owen identifying himself only with those whose personal experience will match his own, but from within the
world and the time of which he partakes. The other poets
of this group tend to be more obviously personal poets
while at the same time echoing Auden's disillusionment
with world affairs, and the 'immeasurable grief' into
which war has plunged civilisation. Spender in *Poetry
since 1939* tells us 'There was a tendency for the poetry of
Day Lewis, MacNeice and Spender to turn inwards towards a personal subject matter and to avoid the world of
outer events.' We are not concerned here with those
strictly personal poems, only with the ones in which the
poets strive to express to the world its own tragedy. And
there are several in which we see the poets seeking to find
an outlet not only for their feelings about war, but for the

[1] 'Autumn Sequel' (1954).
[2] 'The Voyage'.

need they always had to explain the age to itself. That is perhaps why we have so many poems on the raiding and burning of London. In that they could see the need of the people around them and through poetry alone could find some means of transcending the pity of it.

> But words there must be, wept on the crater'd present
> To gleam beyond it.[1]

They tend, moreover, to be poetic journalists in their awareness of contemporary events. 'Autumn Sequel' is full of radio reports, Spender writes of a particular air-raid or of a particular period in Vienna, Auden writes of Nanking, Dachau, of how we've seen

> Old Russia suddenly mutate
> Into a proletarian state.[2]

Every age has had its contemporary references, and most of our finest poets have, if not always written journalistic accounts of current affairs, at least addressed themselves to an audience aware of them. It is quite fitting that of all modern writers on the war, it should be these social-minded poets of the '30s who leave a similar record of their times.

While they are intent on summing up their period and on laying their finger on the very spot that is going to make the rest of the body writhe, they cannot help expressing their horror. Day Lewis's view of his world is

> a day of monsters, a desert of abject stone
> Whose outward terrors paralyse the will.[3]

To express their age in terms of their age, phychological analysis is typical of this group of writers. We have seen how singularly capable Auden is of revealing the

[1] 'Word Over all' (1943).
[2] 'New Year Letter'.
[3] 'The Image' (*Word Over All*).

movement of thought behind the superficial aspect of
civilisation by the very fact that the surface atmosphere is
kept up:

> The lights must never go out
> The music must always play.

There is both analysis of society as a mass-consciousness,
and analysis of the typed individual, the representative of
layers of that society. MacNeice gives us 'The Conscript'
and 'The Mixer', Spender again gives us 'The Conscript',
also the society woman and her son in 'The Fates',
Lehmann imagines what the thoughts of the victor might
be when the present is crowned with laurels and the past
with blood ('Campaign Photograph').

We shall find in these poets the effect of war upon
men's minds, and the guilt it creates. War, they prove, can
become a personal neurosis as tormenting as sex, and it is
interesting to note how, once war comes to the foreground
it takes pride of place as a social evil. It is still the outward
view of world purgatory, even while the poets include
themselves in the picture and while they deal with the
details that disgust the individual. Eric and Anna are seen
not as hero and heroine of 'On the Frontier' – they are
victims. The two primary emotions connected with the
neurosis of war are agony and fear. Day Lewis expresses
it in terms of sickness, but the sickness is itself part of the
neurosis:

> Now Fear has come again
> To live with us
> In poisoned intimacy like pus,
> Hourly extending the area of our pain.

Rarely could an ode have been written that had more
bearing upon its age than this particular 'Ode to Fear'.[1]

It is due to this psychological probing of these poets,

---

[1] *Word Over All.*

that when we have finished reading their poetry we feel
we have been through the war and hated every moment of
it. We have been sick, crazed, paralysed, and frightened –
we have seen the dead, the mad, the fearful, and 'the face
of destruction'. We have seen little of actual warfare, only
of the world in a state of war, and we have cared about
that part of war that goes on after the ravaging – the
murdered village, the dead

> Like effigies thrown down after a fête,[1]

the roofless old, and the child beneath the débris. We
have had it proved to us that war does not pay. And we
are struck most of all by the fact that everything has been
tainted by the war, the marks are left, are exposed, and
are not to be forgotten. *An Italian Visit* was not published until 1953, but as late as this, in the 'Dialogue at
the Airport' there are some enlightening lines on the terms
in which war has made people think, and in which they
will go on thinking for a long time to come – like Lady
Macbeth they cannot erase the stain of blood from the
mind:

> But even you have been taught the simpler associations –
> For example, mouth and famine, lily and corpse, bambino
> And bomb – to say nothing of *odi et amo* – which stand in
>   the light of
> Enjoyment pure and simple.

But apart from the psychology of war, or perhaps as
part of it, we find in these poets the details of everyday
life that brings the war years vividly back to mind. Day
Lewis has one or two poems on the simple folk he knew,
the farmer he fire-watched with, and in 'The Stand-To',
'the ragtag fighters of lane and shadow'. But it is in Louis
MacNeice that we get closest to the atmosphere, thoughts,
and way of life that pervaded the 1940 decade as might

[1] 'The Dead' (*Word Over All*).

be expressed in any newspaper or radio report of the time.
In 'Autumn Sequel' the poet looks back on how

> The war flowed by
> In short or medium waves with a disarray

> Of initials, M.I.5., O.W.I.,
> Of names, Metaxas or Mihailovitch,
> Of doubts and queries, If and But and Why,

> Provided and Supposing, Where and Which,
> And most especially When: oh when would this
> Thing start or that thing stop?

Between 'Autumn Journal' in 1938, which shows the
signs of approaching war, and 'Autumn Sequel' in 1954,
in which life in the after-war years is reviewed, there are
a vast number of short poems which capture the life of our
time in miniature. MacNeice is at ease in a social world –
an urbane poet, he understands without employing or re-
quiring depth, the way certain men were reacting in time
of war —

> Those Haves who cannot bear making a choice,
> Those Have-nots who are bored with having nothing to
> choose.[1]

A poem like 'Swing Song' seems as pointless as war itself,
and suggests that the poet is deliberately seeking after the
common touch. It means that his poetry must remain on
a surface level. Because it is going deliberately to deal
with ordinary people, it must tell us that people are ordinary. In 'Tam Cari Capitis', the reason why we miss someone lies

> in killing
> Time when he could have livened it.

'Autumn Journal' shows us how men were thinking on
the brink of war, how they were living on the banks of

[1] 'Alcohol' (*Collected Poems 1925–48*).

Rubicon, how they were arguing (though superficially it appears the poet's personal argument because he assumes for himself the position of the common man) that the nightmare of history repeating itself can't be really true. On the near side of the war, 'Autumn Sequel' has recorded for future ages the anti-climax in the years following 1945, how although things were gradually returning to what they had been before the war, there still remained a sense of inadequacy

> As usual, Devlin sang
> Folksongs, the Farmer's Boy and the Bold Drover
>
> And the Foggy Dew, but they had lost their tang
> Not being heard in danger.

MacNeice can reflect the doubts and fears of men on a more immediate and less tragic scale than Auden. The sense of insecurity within the changing universe for instance, is related to a similar example taken from classical times

> that all things are mixed
> Or have two sides had taught Thucydides
> How little, a precious little, in life is fixed.

It is an example of a single man, not of a whole universe, of life on a small scale, not on a big one. Perhaps because he keeps so much more closely to an everyday surface life than most of the poets within this group at this particular time, he shares also in the eternal optimism and common-sense view of the man in the street:

> Meanwhile we
> Are here, not There; if we have lost a pawn
>
> We have kept our queen, this is still land, not sea,
> Still life, not death.

Where we really encounter those forces of 'Thrones, Dominions, Powers' etc. in the work of MacNeice is in a radio drama, *The Dark Tower*, which as a piece of 'quest' literature deals more obviously with general and ultimate values. The poet refuses in his Introduction to reveal any intended meaning the play might have, but we don't have to listen for very long before we are aware that it is a parable on our own day and age:

> All that we know is there is something there
> Which makes the Dark Tower dark and is the source
> Of evil through the world. It is immortal
> But men must try to kill it – and keep on trying
> So long as we would be human.

This was broadcast in 1946, a year after the great battle to prevent a deadly menace spreading. It deals with the old legend of Roland whose destiny is to follow his forefathers and his brothers in a search for the Dark Tower, there to face up to the Evil that inhabits it. The whole thing is given a modern connotation. The phrase that Roland has to translate is *Per ardu ad astra*. There is a hint of the soldiers who went out to fight with the knowledge of a previous carnage a bare twenty years before:

> We had a word 'honour' – but it is obsolete.
> Try the word 'duty', and there's another word –
> 'necessity'.

This is not the sole interpretation of *The Dark Tower* – it is a myth that refuses any exact rendering, it is only necessary to point out its significance for our time, the period of the darkness, of 'the age of the dragon' as Lehmann called it. At the end of the play Roland comes across a stone bearing the inscription:

> To Those Who Did Not Go Back –
> Whose Bones being Nowhere, their signature is for All Men –
> Who went to their Death of their Own Free Will
> Bequeathing Free Will to Others.

The Dark Tower is a piece of imaginative literature a little different from the usual descriptive or satirical writings of MacNeice. It approximates more closely to the work of Spender and Lehmann. In 'Returning to Vienna 1947'[1] Spender writes:

> I saw there in our gaze what breaks the heart –
> The tears and bloodshot vein of seeing
> The outer world destroy the inner world.

In these two poets we find continual emphasis laid on the relationship between the two worlds. In Lehmann there is a kind of quiet garden within that cannot be touched by the ravages of war though he is continually aware of it. In his autobiography *The Whispering Gallery* he quotes from a poem showing the signs of approaching war and continues: 'The sense of something in human life indifferent to its great secular dramas and disasters, that crept into the irony of this poem, was classically expressed by Auden in his poem of Breughel's crucifixion. . . .'

Then he goes on to speak of his feeling for the indifference of Nature and quotes:

> All this expanse of noiseless growth, and rock,
> Would hardly stir or change, though just beyond
> World reeled in war's first shock.

Throughout Lehmann's poetry we find nature either as a background or woven into the imagery so that we never lose sight of that quiet garden of his. 'The Sphere of Glass' tells us how brother and sister walking through a wood are protected from the fears of the world by some power linking the grief of the past

> With voices of their vaster war.

In 'Poem'[2] which starts very much like any critical analysis of our present-day life by this group of poets:

[1] *The Edge of Being* (1949).
[2] *The Age of the Dragon* (1951).

> Yes, we are desperate men: our violence,
> The blood that streams from our satanic creeds . . .

the poet at the same time pictures himself stamping through a frosty winter's morning, thinking as he goes

> Such dark thoughts: while I ponder where they flow,
> The winter sun behind the orchard trees
> Has drawn blue shadows on the diamond snow.

Lehmann is closer, as we shall find later, to the younger poets in his manner of writing than to those of his own generation. This is due partly to the language and imagery he draws upon. Where he copies his own generation, he copies their early work: 'The Summer Story'[1] for instance displays all the early Audenesque adventure vocabulary – 'cable, journey, quests, explorer, lake, comrades, citadel'. The thoughts of the group are often echoed in his work, the sense that we have been a race of promise that never proved its worth:

> Far in the censored oceans you are lost,
> But lost the world, too, which your longing haunts.[2]

and at times the horror of the age we live in seizes the poet, where

> in a monstrous rhythm before our eyes
> The alien future, horrible, is born.

Usually his poetry does not rely on political or contemporary reference, but while employing past traditions, literary or historical, is written for our time rather than about it. Poems like 'The Last Ascent', 'The Nightmare', 'There is a house', discuss the age in terms which cannot be nailed down to it. Instead of realistic exactness, the clever hitting of the nail on the head that we find in Auden and MacNeice, we have imaginative distortion. In 'The

---

[1] *The Age of the Dragon* (1951).
[2] 'Letters' (*The Age of the Dragon*).

Nightmare', the poet pictures himself running from the calamities that seek to overwhelm him, and there is one image that could be said to render in literary terms the war dead

> And there were giant statues black as jet
> Prone at my feet.[1]

In a series of articles under the title 'The Armoured Writer'[2] Lehmann suggests there is a change from the 'realist movement' of the '30s; writers are turning more towards symbolism, but at the same time they will still be aware of the age: 'There can be no going back to purely esoteric literature, except among those who are entirely out of touch with the life of their time.'

On the other hand in the modern world 'there is no true and complete picture of existence in which the unseen, what lies beyond our five senses and logical proof, does not play a part'.

Spender's work bears a certain resemblance to Lehmann's in his ability to write of war in terms that are not entirely to do with it. In *The New Realism* (1939) he speaks of how unsatisfactory naturalism has become. There must be an analytic approach to life for the artist must not cut himself off, but – 'Considering the world today as we know it, evidently the analytic approach required must be sweeping, profound and general.' His emphasis is very much upon the inner life, not just its existence, but the necessity for clinging on to it. Though war damages, we must keep alive to the fact of war around us, must learn what suffering teaches.

> To steel the will against awareness would banish
> The angel . . . .
> . . . .

[1] 'The Nightmare' (*The Age of the Dragon*).
[2] *New Writing and Daylight*, Summer 1942.

> Who warns that power, fear, agony, are the life under
>   many;
> That the real is the terrible; that to deny
> This, unsheathes tyranny.[1]

Spender's work at this period expresses a particular kind of agony. There is some bitterness at the thought of how the world after the First World War has plunged itself into another, as in 'The Conscript' and 'June 1940', and he has a feeling comparable with Day Lewis that

> The greater wrong must meet
> From the less evil with the worse defeat.[2]

In fact in *Poetry since 1939* he tells us that many poets were doubtful whether the war was being fought for a purified cause. This increases the agony at the thought of the innocent suffering, because there seems no sufficient explanation for it. In *Trial of a Judge* the evil was quite clearly seen for what it was. But in a poem like 'The War God' there is a bewildered age-old questioning why the wheat cannot be divided and the soldier sent home, why in fact there need be war at all. The poet answers with an analysis of power and revenge, how they go on endlessly in a vicious circle. The title itself is a primitive term for the modern dictator and serves to emphasise the timelessness of the theme. In *New Writing and Daylight*[3] Spender tells us

> The problem of the contemporary writer of any poetry that deals with the struggle of the whole society against external evils is the same as Milton's. He can accept the evil at its face value, but the good has to be created and maintained against the very forces which are fighting the evil.

[1] 'The Angel' (*The Edge of Being*, 1949).
[2] 'June 1940' (*Collected Poems*, 1955).
[3] Winter 1942–3 ('The Creative Spirit II').

The answer to the muddleheadedness of the First World War was attack – irony, sarcasm, criticism of the men at home. But the Second World War was different – the fault could be pinned down to no one in particular, therefore the criticism had to centre upon what we had failed to do rather than upon what we had done. 'The Fates' is a criticism of the shallow strata in which we rested for so long, refusing to recognise that such a reality as war could ever exist, unable to realise that

> History is a dragon under human skin.[1]

The way the poets of this generation deal with the riddle of war is to see it in its context. Spender tells us that the First World War poets like Owen and Sassoon failed in two ways, firstly because they see only the soldier's point-of-view, instead of, like Hardy, seeing the statesman's as well. Therefore it is difficult to say whether Owen and Sassoon were against the war itself (apart from the suffering of the soldiers) because they do not take the reasons for it into account. Their second failure is again their unfairness, because they blame the men at home simply because they are at home (where someone had to be!). 'The limitations of their view of the last war are borne out by the subsequent writings of the soldier poets who survived it.' That is, says Spender, they were not interested in the forces that produced suffering. The modern writer, on the other hand, must be aware, like the Russians, of his background.

We might say that this generation of writers did or tried to do two things in their expression of a war age. They tried to come to grips with the idea of war, with its consequences and its meaning for the human race. Secondly, part of the flavour of these poets lies in their recapturing of the background against which they wrote. We have considered Lehmann's nature imagery, but in

[1] June 1930.

other poets also we are aware of the time of year. 'June 1940' captures the holiday atmosphere in the midst of noises and echoes of war:

> And the grey First War voices, each to each
> Speak, adrift on deck chairs.

We cannot perhaps appreciate in our present position how much of the war years these poets did set down in their work for future generations to read. But they do primarily what might be expected of Second World War poets, discuss the nature of their times. We are meant to think when we read their work, to try to understand ourselves, our position, and the world we live in. To do this they use their personal experience – an air raid, a visit to Vienna, fire-watching, and often an analysis of the way other people think. Demetrios Capetenakis in 'Notes on some Contemporary Writers'[1] reviews the efforts of the '30s poets, and sees them as picturing humanity now 'More complete, deeper, as if with one more dimension, the metaphysical one' quoting Spender's 'Fates', the end of 'The Ambitious Son', 'Elegy', and Lehmann's last poems, 'Summer Story' and 'Vigils'.

[1]*New Writing and Daylight*, 1943.

CHAPTER SEVEN

1939
The Younger Generation of Poets

IT is to this group that we must turn for our 'fighter' poets, the men who correspond to Owen and Sassoon, Grenfell and Brooke, during the First World War, the men who left home to go out and meet the dragon. In it, therefore, we shall include poets like Fuller who belong to Auden's generation in time but who are better classed among the fighters.

On approaching these writers who were at the centre of the aggressive rather than defensive warfare, we might well feel that we are nearing the heart of the matter. They are the men who go through the fire, and the poetry they write will be hot from the furnace. The First World War had been heralded by a stream of propagandist verse – the 'voice of the nation' had celebrated war in its ideal state both at the beginning and also later in its epitaphs. But we have seen how war's glorification was played out among the soldier-poets before the disillusioning years of peace that followed 1918. The Second World War differed from the First both in the kind of war it was and in the spirit in which men approached it. The initial wave of enthusiasm that had inspired not only Julian Grenfell but the young Wilfred Owen as well, did not exist for the Second World War fighters. In *New Writing and Daylight*, 1942–3, Spender writes:

> People marvel that while our young men can go bravely to their deaths, they cannot write heroic patriotic war poetry. It is greatly to their credit that they do not do so. They are willing to give their lives for the cause of the

democracies, but not to tell heroic lies. In that dis-
crimination lies a greater hope for the future than lay
with the generation of Rupert Brooke.[1]

All generalisations about the Second World War poetry
must of course be qualified and taken to refer to 'the
majority of poems'. The bulk of poetry was so huge that
there may well be at least one exception to every statement made on it.

The Second World War as I have said, differed from
the First in kind, being a war not of men, but which involved men. There were many forms of death – by bomb
shells, by explosion, by drowning, by fire, by gas – but the
day of trenches and bayonets was fast becoming obsolete
and hand to hand fighting was reserved for the few. Personal contact with the enemy during the First World War
had perpetuated some vestiges of chivalry that no longer
existed during the Second. Robert Graves pin-pointed the
distinction in a comment on how the Germans behaved
during the 1914–18 conflict:

> On the whole, they fought fairly and courageously; and
> I felt most grateful, after Loos, when they held their fire
> and allowed us to get our wounded in from no-man's
> land. 'Kaiser Bill' might deserve hanging as Lloyd
> George claimed, but he was no Hitler. The need to
> regard Hitler's Nazis as a horde of criminal lunatics
> robbed war of its few remaining decencies, and the idea
> of fraternising with them would have been ridiculous
> from the very start.[2]

During the Second World War there was a great divorce
between enemy and enemy, with men incarcerated in
their machines – aeroplanes, tanks, ships, submarines – an
unnatural, impersonal, and monstrous form of warfare,
culminating in the atomic bomb. Moreover, men's lives

[1] 'The Creative Spirit II'.
[2] *Observer*, November 9th, 1958.

had to be organised and regimented, as part of the vast machinery of war. There could be analysed

> A growing self-detachment making man
> Less homesick, fearful, proud,
> But less a man[1]

In this century war has become the proudest product of a machine age. Not the poet only, but the novelist and the dramatist have been caught up in mirroring the retreat from nature, and the change forced upon man himself by his 'progress'. Over and over again in writers such as Shaw, Huxley, Waugh, Orwell, we find that not only are men's thoughts perverted but the 'natural' instincts and forms of life are mass-organised and re-distributed – sex, physical attributes, home life, birth, even death, are reduced to a scientific level that makes a primitive life seem to produce the noble savage.

The reaction of the younger generation of poets writing during the actual period of fighting is an interesting one, for the evils of warfare suddenly become side issues compared with the eternal themes of Love, Separation, and Death. For what, in a world of science and mass sadism, the Second World War poets were concerned with was 'men as they are men within themselves'.

Firstly they wrote about themselves, and secondly they wrote for the people around them who they knew felt the same. In a way they found it a necessity to preserve something personal and something that might outlast their own transience. History had already shown them the fate of 'the common soldier' as simply 'grey stone in a field of green'.[2] They have a continual awareness of their own youth, of having 'hardly started to suck the core of the apple'[3] and above all, of never perhaps having the opportunity.

[1] Alun Lewis, 'After Dunkirk' (*Raiders' Dawn*, 1942).
[2] John Bayliss, 'October'.
[3] Alan Rook, 'War Generation' (*Soldiers this Solitude*).

> the lilies of ambition
> still spring in their climate, still unpicked:
> but time, time is all I lacked
> to find them, as the great collectors before me.[1]

These poets are aware as much as Owen was that they are speaking for a war generation, but theirs is not so much a desire to tell the world what it already knew only too well, but to get from life on the spot the things they most wanted:

> living each hour on the crumbs of a bargain broken,
> ignoring the haemorrhage.[2]

This was an attitude common to many people during the instability of the war years. On a practical everyday level it could be seen in the on-the-spot marriages, the black market, the grabbing of everything that could be got while it could be got. Rupert Brooke had idealised the things he loved as worth dying for. The second generation of war poets wanted to possess those things once again before they died. Their poetry is a history of the struggle to retain and the struggle to give up. In the final event they had to face death 'Knowing I am no lover, but destroyer.'[3]

This continual conflict enriches their poetry in two ways. The life they loved had a heightened attraction by its sudden desirability – and the necessity for turning away from it, the necessity for growing into a different kind of person without losing the old one, involved the growth of spiritual vision. The diamond had not only to be polished, it had to be cut to a different shape.

Ronald Wilcox's 'Operational Squadron'[4] shows how

[1] Keith Douglas, 'On a return from Egypt' (*Collected Poems* 1964).

[2] Alan Rook, 'War Generation'.

[3] Sidney Keyes, 'The Wilderness' (*Collected Poems*, 1945).

[4] *Air-Force Poetry* (1946).

the poet is aware of what is taking place among his generation. He feels the sudden blazing awareness of life:

> Suddenly life leaps up to a swift crescendo,
> a taut fatality hangs upon the days
> so scarcely left to us.

To balance this hailing of life, there is the leave-taking
(speaking for a generation whose *Ave atque Vale* must be
spoken in the same breath).

> Now we have said farewell to loveliness,
> to quietude, the cool unhurried dreams
> and quiet aspirations; all that seems
> fantastic now, for we have seen the cess
> this world is built on.

The war was, after all, a struggle for existence – for the
preservation of a whole system of values because it stood
for a way of life and thought that the Nazi régime was set
on stamping out. The poets suggest that it was fought less
with the feeling that there was something to hate than with
the resolve that there should be something left to love:

> It was not red resolve of anger stole the young
> Nor even hate:
> But love of living, O very bounty of love,
> Into their open hearts aimed irons of fate.[1]

We need not therefore expect to find poetry dealing
with the enemy, or even inferring any enemy except 'the
world'. Anything on the Huns, Attila, Mussolini, or Hitler
is completely ruled out. The iron had not entered so
deeply into their soul as it had into that of the older generation who had seen the German menace twice over. In
'Graves: El Alamein', Pudney can suggest that we live and
let live, and not harbour bitterness against the foe that fell
with us.

[1] John Pudney, 'In the dark nature of forgiveness' (*Commemorations*).

The feeling, however, of having been pushed into a war not of their own choosing is probably the chief source of bitterness, as far as bitterness does show itself in their work. Sometimes it is a direct outcry like Keyes's 'War Poet', reminiscent of Wilfred Owen:

> I am the man who looked for peace and found
> My own eyes barbed.

Sometimes it emerges in a rather acid humour like Fuller's account of the various pains and disabilities of poets from Blake's madness to Southwell's hanging, ending

> I envy not only their talents
> And fertile lack of balance
> But the appearance of choice
> In their sad and fatal voice.[1]

Or to sink to the bottom of the scale, there is Charles Causley's 'Soldiers Chorus'[2] on the lad being called up:

> Say that you did it for glory
>   Defending your hoary name
> It's still the same bloody old story
>   And I'm pushed in the pit just the same.

On the whole, these poets make no attempt to remedy the situation – they are neither social thinkers, nor satirists. Though there is one outstanding exception to this, Alex Comfort, whose poetry gives us an impression of him, not merely as a satirist, but as an idealist intent upon saying 'This must not happen again, because this need not happen again':

> There is one freedom only –
> to take the hands of men called enemies
> and you and they walking together go
> to seek out every throat that told you Kill.[3]

The Signal to Engage, the volume containing this poem

---

[1] 'January 1940 (*The Middle of a War*).
[2] *Survivor's Leave* (1958).
[3] 'Song for the Dead' (*The Signal to Engage*).

which pointed out that victory could be dead-sea fruit, was published in 1946, directly after the war, when memories of war and loss of men, and the animal state to which many lives had been reduced (seen especially with the freeing of prisoners-of-war) were uppermost in men's minds – a period when we could start actually thinking about what had happened, survey the damage and start the clearing up. At the same time it was a period of memorials, of concluding speeches, of welcoming the soldiers home and burying the dead – it was no less than a return to 1918. 'We live in a blind time' points the irony of the age:

> the animals that feed from communal graves
> going about chewing and saying Victory, Freedom,
> Justice, then turning for another mouthful.

Probably the bitterest and most ironic poetry was produced at the conclusion of the war, once the atom bomb had been let loose (cf. Edith Sitwell's 'Shadow of Cain', Auden's 'Shield of Achilles', D. J. Enright's 'The Monuments of Hiroshima', Pudney's 'Commemorations'). Comfort is resolved that the living must go on fighting a different kind of battle now, for their dead comrades' sake:

> for never before the circle of time threw up
> such battle as we join, nor ranged so clearly
> men against government, sent a resistless voice
> saying to all who still live – choose: to the dead – Silence![1]

Some of Comfort's poetry, especially 'We live in a blind time', is reminiscent of First World War poetry. But compared with the bulk of Comfort's work, the amount is slight. It differs also in suggesting that a course of action be taken rather than seeking to arouse either pity or horror at the extravagance of war. 'At a meeting in a garden' puts into symbolic form the resolution to end war – from

[1] 'Song for the Dead' (*The Signal to Engage*).

a hill top the poet decides that History will be defeated because

> we will go down
> to make the level countryside spring out
> in many-coloured fire, as we fight
> and snap the backs of those who killed our friends.[1]

In one way Comfort resembles the middle generation of poets, in putting forward the need for a concerted effort on behalf of a whole society. 'The Petrified Forest', for instance, has echoes of the Fascist régime and its 'yes-men'. And in 'Children in the Luxembourg Gardens', there is the appeal to the 'fellow student' to understand the picture of dead children as a matter of principle.

Yet the attiude of most of the other young writers is that of Alun Lewis when he mentions 'the world we could not change'.[2] They are only too aware that they are victims, not partakers of the political situation, as bewildered as young children cast off by their mother for no apparent reason. In 'Home Thoughts from Abroad',[3] Lewis says exactly this of the West —

> We surely were not hard to please
> And yet you cast us out.

It is characteristic of the young soldier generation as opposed to the intellectual of the period, that the world situation should be simply background for the personal. It comes out clearly in Lewis's 'The Island'[4] where the poet addresses the young patrician leaving his tiny home so proudly for the mainland:

> And do you in this piteous human flux
> Possess the high imponderable art
> To turn us by a hair's breadth in our trouble
> To greater agony or joy of heart?

[1] *The Signal to Engage.*
[2] 'The Jungle' (*Ha! Ha! among the trumpets,* 1945).
[3], [4] *Ha! Ha! among the trumpets.*

The majority of young poets speak for the men like them involved in the same situation. Because the plight is a common one, the voice of the poet speaking personally,

> Remember me when I am dead
> and simplify me when I'm dead.[1]

becomes identifiable with all the others who are silent.

'This piteous human flux' sums up the poetry of this generation. In Roy Fuller we find echoes of the '30s – mention of Spain, of how civilisation has been affected, of History as a living, breathing force (as also in Comfort), but even Fuller feels the pull of something apart from 'the situation'. In 'The Statue'[2] he conveys a sense of human values not dependent upon war. The statue of a warrior itself epitomises the war, the purpose, the cause – history in the making. But imposing as it is, it must take second place beside the memory of a man smoking a pipe, contemplating his great dirty feet —

> As though there dominated this sea's threshold and this night
> Not the raised hooves, the thick snake neck, the profile, and the might,
> The wrought, eternal bronze, the dead protagonist, the fight,
> But that unmoving, pale but living shape that drops no tears,
> Ridiculous and haunting, which each epoch reappears,
> And is what history is not. O love, O human fears!

The poets of this generation try to apprehend that part of human life which is timeless, but they pinpoint man in a certain kind of situation, man as he is affected emotionally and spiritually by a war age.

If they are not primarily concerned with man as a

[1] 'Simplify me when I'm dead', Keith Douglas.
[2] *A Lost Season* (1944).

political animal, have these young poets opinions about
the war itself? First and foremost they realise, young as
they are, that this war is different from the others and
therefore cannot be expressed in the same terms because

> the words for honour and glory
> Wear too small.[1]

Together with this goes the awareness that this generation
itself is different. Apart from the fact that it has been
called to almost certain sacrifice – or possibly because of
it – it is also supremely an earnest generation that has set
itself to a task. Against the existence of war, against the
hardships of war it frequently rebels, but the sacrifice it
accepts.

> For there lies all our power; the power of the young and
> the lonely.
> I know that the past is lies, and the present only
> Important. I see in life service and in dying an end
> Of loving.[2]

They accept their place in the war even though 'Too
undeceived for patriotic man'.[3] It is some of the things war
means that they find hard to stomach and which make for
an underlying bitterness to a great deal of their work.

War is experienced and pictured on three levels. First
there is the burden of war which they themselves must
bear, the separation from home, the boredom, the desire

> To see the worst, and yet not die
> Of their lucid despair.[4]

In Alan Rook it is in as physical terms as Dante's journey
in *The Divine Comedy*:

[1] John Pudney, 'Fall' (*Beyond this Disregard*).
[2] Alan Rook, 'The Retreat' (*Soldiers this Solitude*).
[3] Lawrence Whistler, 'In Time of Suspense' (*Poems of this War*).
[4] David Gascoyne, 'Zero: September 1939'.

Please God teach me how the mountain carries
the weight of heaven; and to run with streams which go
uncomplaining through the weight of their own valleys.[1]

On the second level there is the actual Inferno of war
that must be passed through. This is different from war's
actualities, from the bloodshed and the guns – the latter
belong to a world at war, but the Inferno expressed by
some of these young poets is a kind of Underworld created
by war, where they find

The emptiness of noon, the void of night.[2]

It is difficult to express the presence of this quality in
their work except as spiritual nightmare. John Lehmann
has pointed out that 'the void is Fuller's dominating experience', that his images emphasise 'abdication, loss, deception, degradation.'[3] But he is not alone in his feeling
for this emptiness. The following passage from Alun Lewis
is superficially an account of the horrors of warfare, but
read again, those horrors become themselves images
building up an atmosphere not of destruction but something far nearer to Dante's Inferno – a state where these
things go on endlessly, where hope is lost 'that comes to
all'. The poet is keeping vigil, waiting in the barracks for
his love – who does not come.

And here the hiatus falls, the stammer,
The black-lipped wound that mouths oblivion,
Here children scream and blood is shed in vain
In a dark eclipse where the shadowy mistral blinds
Our daunted eyes and touches us to dust.[4]

In Alan Rook it takes an even more abstract and arid
form when he speaks of

[1] 'The Task' (*We who are fortunate*, 1945).
[2] Alun Lewis, 'Infantry' (*Ha! Ha! among the trumpets*).
[3] *New Writing and Daylight*, Autumn 1944 (The Armoured
Writer V').
[4] 'War Wedding', I – The Vigil (*Raiders' Dawn*).

> the indifferent phrase
> and gesture of the ugly, the long-neglected
> vision of love which created only
> a wider loneliness.[1]

The third form that war takes is the actual day-to-day realities, strangely enough at first sight the least dwelt on, except in a certain class of poetry. There are always many kinds of poetry produced during a war. If we look for journalistic accounts we are more likely to find them in barrack room ballad literature or imitation of the barrack room ballad, and even then it is confined to mess-life rather than dealing with the large-scale horrors of machine warfare.

It is said that we have probably learnt more about day-to-day life in the forces than any generation previous to Kipling. Yet the poems dealing with this must not be taken as mere soldiers' reminiscences, many are more professional than that, written by men who were unusually sensitive to 'the inevitable adjective', and who usually either expressed or conveyed disgust or hatred or boredom at men sitting together

> Bound by no ideal of service
> But by a common interest in pornography and a desire to
>   outdrink one another.[2]

This was the life encountered by young men, as the rest of the poem shows, still with some ideal of living life to the full by being ready

> To draw my last breath
> Amidst a chaos of dramatic thunder,

In Kenneth Neal's picture of army life, he is forced to cry

> Let us have some clean killing at the last !

. . . .

[1] 'Poem from H.Q.' (*Soldiers this Solitude*).
[2] Timothy Corsellis 'What I never saw' (*Poems of this war*).

> It's mad – the stupid and the humble folk
> Are khaki heroes here, the beautiful's a swear
>   Word and our lives a dirty joke.[1]

That other aspect of day-to-day reality we might expect, the large-scale horrors of extensive warfare, does enter Second World War poetry but it enters in a special way. Although most poets refrain from sitting down deliberately to write of events or situations involving fighting, the themes of Love, Separation, and Death are often related in terms of war. The imagery in Keyes's 'A hope for those separated by war', is almost entirely drawn from a fund of 'outrages'. In Keith Douglas there is the dwelling upon the physical horror of rotting flesh and bone as in much of 1914–18 poetry, but within this poet's vision it becomes part of a universal ravage of death upon life, of time upon growth, of a process in which war plays only a part. His landscapes are made up of a fusion of the natural and the man-made, with nature triumphing in the end:

> the vegetation is of iron
> dead tanks, gun barrels split like celery
> the metal brambles have no flowers or berries
> and there are all sorts of manure, you can imagine
> the dead themselves, their boots, clothes and possessions
> clinging to the ground.[2]

Yet when poets turn to writing on such subjects as an attack on Malta or the occupation of France, where realism might well be expected, the opposite is true of their imagery. The coming of war in Alex Comfort's 'France'[3] is related in the following terms:

> – There are doors opened where no doors were,
> The cradle's gone. The slim chimneys are fallen.

[1] 'Army' (*Poems of this war*).
[2] 'Cairo Jag'.
[3] *A Wreath for the Living*.

On the military side it is not so much the fighting that seems to affect poets as the thought of war in terms of large-scale 'horror': the fact that this has been planned and organised, that it is so completely impersonal, and that innocent people are involved in it. Here we might note the exception of the air-force fighters. For them there was something of the exhilaration that Grenfell found in battle – even in fear. There is something above the sordid and the horrible and the painful about

> This infinite upon whose little rim
> Man dares to crawl.[1]

Spender in *Poetry since 1939* speaking of Blunden and Sassoon as 'circumscribed', considers how the poets of this war will compare: 'Probably their development will be different because this war, with all its terrors, has been adventurous and expansive, more likely to produce agoraphobia than the claustrophobia of the war 1914–18.'

The chief of our air-force poets was John Pudney, and he, in spite of an underlying bitterness, manages to capture the heroics and thrill of flying – not always in poems actually on the subject of the part the air force played during the war, but in the slight romanticism of his imagery, and in his conception of war on an abstract rather than wholly concrete level. In 'Rank and File'[2] he celebrates Rodrigo de Triano who accompanied Christopher Columbus, and died at sea,

> not for a tale to be told
> Of America, Europe or gold,
> But because the eye is wide and blood is red.

Let us return to the point made at the beginning, that on the whole the poets deliberately accepted the part they

---

[1] O. C. Chave, 'There are no frontiers in the sky' (*Air-Force Poetry*).

[2] *Beyond this Disregard.*

were allotted in war. We find two things resulting. It means in the first place that they turned to face something at an early age that youth isn't usually called upon to face. While life was still at the full they had to enter what Keyes called 'The Wilderness'. This is pictured as a spiritual state apart from day-to-day reality, that inevitably employs symbols for its expression. Keyes's poem is the finest example of this, with its insistence both on the harshness of the country he must pass through and the necessity for continuing:

> Here where the horned skulls mark the limit
> Of instinct and intransigent desire
> I beat against the rough-tongued wind
> Towards the heart of fire.

There is a connection with some of the symbolic works of the middle generation, especially in the theme of a journey. But to the young poets the theme has turned into a direct personal experience.

> We do not know the end, we cannot tell
> That valley's shape, nor whether the white fire
> Will blind us instantly....
>   Only we go
> Forward, we go forward together, leaving
> Nothing except a worn-out way of loving.[1]

In Alun Lewis's 'Sacco writes to his Son' we have a more down-to-earth expression of stoicism:

> Be not perturbed if you are called to fight
> Only a fool thinks life was made his way.

The other side to the poets' acceptance of war is hope, that by leaving what they desire they are giving something to the future, that it is the life they leave that is the justification for their leaving it:

[1] Sidney Keyes, 'The Wilderness'.

> For young and old who die
> At every hour
> Now life is sole and solemn monument.[1]

They are occupied frequently with speaking for their generation before it perishes, with the feeling that it will perish, and that they wish us to know why they have accepted their fate:

> Whatever happens, remember we strove for a more beautiful world.[2]

In the First World War there had been a feeling after a while that men were dying for no apparent cause, and that patriotism was not enough to justify the wholesale slaughter. The Second World War was of such a nature that patriotism went by the board in the attempt to preserve some part of the world as fit to live in.

What the young poets saw themselves as dying for was certainly not to retain freedom, for they had never actually existed under any kind of tyranny, Fascist or Communist. The Second World War as far as England was concerned began in 1939 and ended in 1945. What was taking place on the continent during the 1930s was, in the eyes of the masses merely what was taking place on the continent. The English, apart from those who travelled abroad, were aware of the Gestapo on the radio, not at their front door. Even Mr. Chamberlain who did travel abroad turned the proverbial blind eye. For a country like Hungary the war never really came to an end. But upon England, there fell like a shot from the blue, six years that could well be described as un-English. Spender's 'The Fates' was not on the whole far short of the mark. As Roy Fuller wrote in his 'Dedicatory Poem' to *Epitaphs and Occasions*

---

[1] John Pudney, 'Memorial' (*Beyond this Disregard*).

[2] Keidrych Rhys 'Letter to my Wife' (*The Van Pool and other poems*).

> For us the Reichstag burned to tones
> Of Bach on hand-made gramophones.
> We saw the long-drawn fascist trauma
> In terms of the poetic drama.

Yet this generation, even without a flag to fly, are neither cynics nor pessimists. Alex Comfort writes of soldiers

> Not fools, but men who knew the price obeying,
> the lice for what they were, the Cause for a fraud,
> hoped for no good and cherished no illusions.[1]

Nor were they by any means de Vigny writers, they did not lose themselves in service. Quite the opposite in fact. The values they appreciate and the values they come to appreciate are outside duty and heroism. They are civilian, not military. Thomas Hardy wrote in 'In time of the breaking of nations' of those things that will always be part of the English landscape. He among all the poets of the First World War, anticipated what was to be the guiding light of the young Second World War poets.

Wherever these young poets were stationed they were calmly sitting down and writing about their particular background – Alun Lewis in India, Roy Fuller in Africa, Alex Comfort in France, John Pudney flying over Malta. They give us a picture of how life went on in various parts of the world during the war —

> Zeppu will forget
> And Grez, barefooted, carrying her shoes,
> Will pray for some till harvest.[2]

Peasants gather in the harvest, strike up their tribal dances, give birth, copulate, and die, in their poetry. There is a width and yet a fundamentalism in their outlook, both of which seem to remove the poets from their

[1] 'Song for the heroes' (*The Signal to Engage*).
[2] John Pudney, 'Malta' (*South of Forty*).

particular time. This is partly due to the kind of civilisation they found themselves amongst. If they had been
writing about a country like England, their thoughts
might have been more securely bounded by war. But
instead they were coming into contact with life and
thought so different from their own, that not even the
exigencies of war could detract from the strangeness of
their travels. Alun Lewis wrote in one of his letters:

> England is easy compared with India – easier to corrupt
> and easier to improve. There are few deterrents at
> home: the inclination isn't continually oppressed by the
> cosmic disinclination, the individual isn't so ruthlessly
> and permanently subject to the laissez faire of the sun
> and the sterility.[1]

The richness and fullness of the life and values these
poets depict may be compared with the poverty of the
First World War realism. They are part of an age for
which the world was becoming easily compassable, an age
that was living in terms of continents and civilisations
rather than countries – partly because of the economic development of new parts of the world, partly because war
stretched much farther afield than it had done previously,
partly because countries like Turkey were being Western-
ised, partly because of the improvement of communica-
tions. Whatever the reason, the extent of the war was
itself indicative of the twentieth-century outlook, and the
poets expressed their feeling for something which existed
outside themselves.

Just as the heroic dramatists of the late seventeenth
century travelled extensively in imagination, creating a
fantasy that spelled in reverse a period gradually seeking
to contain itself within intellectual, civilised bounds, so the
twentieth-century poet in an age that tries hard to be up-
to-date and progressive, finds a release in the historic – but
the history that has actually taken place and is still con-

[1] Introduction to *Ha! Ha! among the trumpets.*

tinuing today, the sense of the past and all its values that remains even in the present. The younger generation of poets captured some of the atmosphere of the traditional beneath the shadow of the Second World War. John Pudney's 'Siege of Malta' presents the people of that country as embodying all the events that have happened to them in the past, and even this war is only one more to add to the centuries of invasion and passing civilisations:

> Phoenician-eyed, these saw Carthage and Rome,
> Greeks, Infidels and Normans in their humours.
>
> . . . .
>   No toll
> Ever was taken but here these eyes looked on,
> And the waters were troubled with blood and oil.
> Death blooms in Mediterranean profusion:
> We are old where nothing is new, now, Airman John.

The poets' outlook on the past is never free of the present, just as the seventeenth-century dramatists were never wholly free from seventeenth-century ideals. In this generation of poets the past shows up those things that are fundamental to any age and yet which are particularly apposite at the time. The poets are thinking in terms of universals – Love, Separation, Death – but at the same time their outlook is that of men involved in a twentieth-century world-wide struggle. In 'The Odyssey' of Alun Lewis the poet pictures the thoughts of a sailor departing from burning Troy, discovering that there is nothing glorious about any of their deeds, that even the leader is afraid of Life:

> We knew that vision of a ruined age
> To be the shape our minds and deeds had fashioned,
> And we ourselves to be a wretched omen
> Tossed in the tides and never making landfall,
> A dying race whose doom it was to live.

The poet could as well have said it about his own destructive generation as about the Greeks. It was a constant reflection of his that he and his comrades were 'Tossed in the tides and never making landfall'.

Likewise Lehmann says of Roy Fuller's African poems, that he uses animal life.

> to point some grim and pitiful truth about the life he and his comrades are leading.[1]

Giraffes, for instance, are remarkable and strange because they are 'creatures walking without pain or love',[2] in a time when, it is implied, these are fundamental beyond everything else to human beings.

Something of an explanation can be found again in a letter of Alun Lewis:

> I've taken a sardonic title for the poems from Job 39. 'Ha! Ha! among the trumpets.' You know the beautiful chapter. The liberty of the wild ass, the lovelessness of the ostrich, the intrepidity of the horse. These are the particulars. The infinite, of which I can never be sure, is God the Maker. I prefer the ostrich's eggs warming in the sun. I avoid speculations and haven't been touched by intuitions.[3]

Here Lewis sums up on his own behalf what we find in nearly all the young poets – the feeling for particular everyday detail as a vehicle for expressing a depth of experience arising from their situation: 'for there doesn't seem to be any question more directly relevant than this one, of what survives of all the beloved.'

Combined with this is a sensitivity to what is natural and what is not. The kind of war that was taking place must have stood out in direct contrast to the background of Nature and life lived according to the dictates of nature. Add to this the dislike of their own position. The result is

[1] *New Writing and Daylight*, Autumn 1944 ('The Armoured Writer V').

[2] 'The Giraffes' (*A Lost Season*).

[3] Introduction to *Ha! Ha! among the trumpets*.

a poetry that harks back to a time of peace, that sees in the soldier's life something unnatural, and considers the years of war as a turning aside from and distortion of the laws of the universe. What is important is that instead of burying themselves in memories of happier times, these poets record for us the joys of a natural life within the setting of their present situation.

Whatever the poet may remember of the beloved, he is aware of change. There is 'A hope for those separated by war' but the lovers must reach each other through and in spite of the tortures they endure. In 'Encirclement'[1] the poet strives through his present surroundings to reach the place

> Where the lamplit room awaits a stranger
> And suffering has sanctified your face.

There is Life going on after the breaking of nations, and spelling hope for the future. These poems are full of the most joyful natural description as opposed to the social satire of the middle generation. Questions are raised, morals are pointed in terms of Nature. David Gascoyne especially is a poet of the English landscape who yet is aware of a war background. 'Snow in Europe' is a poem with many significances. Europeans have their dreams but they cannot stop the snow. Therefore, it implies, they won't stop the flow of blood either. The poet shows how snow has stopped war by glossing over boundaries, but the nations are waiting in readiness for it to disappear. The snow itself is an agent of beauty, and by its very habit of blotting out distinctions an agent of peace – it is only man who is out of his natural element, who sets up his own lines of demarcation and quarrels over them. 'Walking at Whitsun'[2] is more purely a poem of description, turned only at the end into a reminder of war:

[1] *Ha! Ha! among the trumpets.*
[2] David Gascoyne, *Poems 1937–42.*

H

> And meditating as I pace
> The afternoon away, upon the smile
> (Like that worn by the dead) which Nature wears
> In ignorance of our unnatural tears,
> From time to time I think: How such a sun
> Must glitter on their helmets! How bright-red
> Against this sky's clear screen will ruins burn . . .

There is something perennial about the seasons and what they bring with them that is both the hall-mark of a future and an antithesis to a war manufactured by men:

> and still Spring must
> Swing back through Time's continual arc to earth.[1]

When Keyes in 'Cervières' wishes to express the continuance of that which is destroyed, he does it through the image of the cherry orchard despoiled by birds and yet resown because of the life remaining in the seed.

It is this hope for a future life that the poets leave behind them. Nature is often used as an image of all they most value – in Keyes it has literary connotations, the rivers and gardens that are left behind for the wilderness – in Lewis it is a sign that 'We are of Life':[2]

> Only the fleeting sunlight in the forest,
> And dragonflies' blue flicker on quiet pools
> Will perpetuate our vision
> Who die young.

And in Rook it becomes

> a vision so real that almost
> you could squeeze it.[3]

Kathleen Raine wrote in *New Road* (1943) of how poets were once again taking the direct road to aesthetic creation, by selecting the beautiful for their raw material,

[1] Sidney Keyes, 'Cervières'.
[2] Lines on a Tudor Mansion' (*Raiders' Dawn*).
[3] 'Poem from H.Q.' (*Soldiers this Solitude*).

whereas the previous Audenesque fashion had been to achieve conflict between material that reflected the coarse and commonplace world with 'the flame of poetry that transmutes the workaday realism'. She talks of young poets feeling with 'nerves of beauty' as against 'nerves of pain' to suggest this reversal, adding: 'It seems that the war, far from producing a crop of war poetry, has made us turn to life with new reverence.'

We find the feeling for natural beauty acting also upon the poets' desire for home, for their women and their children. Separation is seen as one of the unnatural results of being at war, and the poets celebrate sex in its most natural and erotic form. Previously Wilfred Owen had abandoned all thoughts of the beloved in order to dwell upon the death of his martyred comrades. Occasionally the same thing emerges in Second World War poetry. Keith Douglas writes

> How can I live among this gentle
> obsolescent breed of heroes, and not weep?[1]

But on the whole the Second World War poets were not primarily interested in describing dying men, but in expressing the feelings of men in a similar situation, recognising that

> What's done
> To me is done to many.[2]

Alun Lewis admits that his poems are 'expressions of personal experience' written for his wife Gweno. Time and again he points out that mankind generally, having lost the fine mastery over its fate, has brought about a situation culminating in the poet's separation from the beloved:

> And huge as the shadows
> My longing runs wild

[1] 'Aristocrats'.
[2] Roy Fuller, 'What is terrible' (*A Lost Season*).

> Oh world! Oh wanton!
> For my woman, my child.[1]

The love expressed in these poems is usually very simple and very earthy – it is the soldier's longing for the warmth of his bed and his wife's arms. But its significance for some poets extends further than this. In one 'Song' Lewis tells us —

> That Life has trembled in a kiss
> From Genesis to Genesis,
> And what's transfigured will live on
> Long after Death has come and gone.[2]

Love has the final power in the poems of this generation. Part of it is possibly derived from the abstract expression of the need for love in the poetry of Spender, Auden, and their group, although this sometimes enters also in a similar form among the younger poets. But in them it develops further into a full-blooded yearning for life with all its natural joys. In 'Odi et Amo'[3] the strength of the poet's hatred for war and 'this blood-soaked forest of disease' is contrasted with the strength of his love for forms of life:

> My soul cries out with love
> Of all that walk and swim and fly.
> From the mountains, from the sky,
> Out of the depths of the sea
> Love cries and cries in me.

Separation from the beloved is sometimes a sign that the world is out of its natural state. On the other hand the significance of *amor* may be only in its being a constant aid to the fighter in the midst of warfare, keeping him normal, human, and happy, in a private life that goes on

[1] 'Chanson Triste'.
[2] *Ha! Ha! among the trumpets*.
[3] Alun Lewis, *Raiders Dawn*.

existing through and above all world-wide catastrophe. These poets speak for the individual rather than society, for the Englishman absent from his home rather than England at war.

> O ecstasies of courting days. O clouded quarrel days
> The Fuehrer wants a word with you! the simple life the simple Joy just stays.[1]

Whether these young poets would have been writing love sonnets if the world had been at peace, and whether the war was an intrusion into the poet's personal world, or whether the theme of love arose through the war, it is difficult to say. It seems, however, more likely that the war brought out the personal desires, hopes and frustrations, as much of what they wrote (especially before and since the war) shows an ability to absorb what is outside themselves, even to think in terms of social satire (Pudney, Lewis, Comfort).

They were, however, involved at an early age in action. The immediacy of their experience vitalises both the drama of their work and the sentiments. They themselves realise that the climax of their lives has been forced upon them before they have had time to think about it:

> For what is lost to this
> generation is the passionate withdrawal,
> the consistent retreat to the desert. And what
> has come is the participation
> in the involuntary event.[2]

They are, in fact, recording the position that Auden had prophesied for them in *On the Frontier* when he spoke of the generation that could not stand apart.

The final realisation comes gradually, that resignation to war and to separation eventually means resignation to

[1] Keidrych Rhys, 'Letter to my Wife'.
[2] Alan Rook, 'Poem from H.Q.' (*Soldiers this Solitude*).

death. It means a deliberate and irrevocable abandonment of the things they most value. In the First World War death meant carnage and waste. In the Second it means neither the horrors of bloodshed nor the pitiful throwing away of life. That is too external a form. Above all, it is not enlarged by the imagination, the poets are not going out of their way to play upon our emotions, although they can move us – they are recording an experience. And they achieve an impression of the nearness of death that is hardly to be paralleled:

> I have left
> The lovely bodies of the boy and girl
> Deep in each other's placid arms;
>
> . . . .
>
> I have begun to die
> And the guns' implacable silence
> Is my black interim, my youth and age.[1]

Sidney Keyes was a poet who, once he had become involved in war, wrote as a voice for the life and generation of which he was a part. It is no accident that he tells the voiceless speakers to

> Cry through the trumpet of my rage and fear.

It is significant also, from our findings on what poets were writing about, that his themes embrace both the soldier and the lover. 'The Foreign Gate' for instance enters intimately and sensitively into the pain of separation and the agony of death. Of the experience of death, he tells us:

> Whatever gift, it is the giving
> Remains significant, whatever death
> It is the dying matters.

Whatever form death takes (and that is not the preoccupation of this generation of poets) it is the turning to meet it that raises it to another plane:

[1] Alun Lewis, 'The Sentry' (*Raiders' Dawn*).

> And there the soul found strength
> To break the blurred delirious veils
> Of silence and of pathos and of self.[1]

The poets record various stages in their attitude to the subject. We are not left with the impression that the struggle has been easy, only that on the whole it has been victorious. It is for nearly all of them 'hard and bitter agony', especially at the thought that this generation that has not reached maturity is itself something precious that is being lost to the world:

> Man has not learned, man has not lived,
> And man is dying, in his death
> Godlike as lightning and more ruinous.[2]

The bitterness that arose with the First World War poets is softened in the Second World War poetry partly by acceptance, partly by the thought of the beauty and power of the dark (the poet again feeling with nerves of beauty rather than of pain), partly by the consolation in a poet like Rook that

> death shall come
> not in the moment of expected danger
> but only
> when the reaper is ripe for the corn,[3]

partly because of the level of tragic splendour to which they raise the subject of their final destiny. Gascoyne in his 'Farewell Chorus' sees it as the culminating point of

> 'Years through the rising storm of which we grew,'

realising that all the petty fears and trivialities of those years are falling away, leaving them with certain truths about men's lives.

---

[1] Alun Lewis, 'Parable' (*Raiders' Dawn*).
[2] Clifford Dyment, 'Now is the Fall' (*Collected Poems 1935–48*).
[3] 'Harvest' (*These are my comrades*).

Beyond despair
May we take wiser leave of you, knowing disaster's cause.

But the dominant mood is one that is common to every-body involved in the war, at home or abroad – the ex-pectation of death at any moment as something life is now bringing – forging a bond between all men because of the mortality they have in common:

you will be quiet, all of you –
quiet, in rows; for this city is dropping its cones,
life is dropping its cones, and they roll, and we are among
them.[1]

The First World War in 1914 celebrated its young men going out to fight heroically for cause and country, and in 1918 it exalted its dead. The Second World War does very little of either. In fact there is a continual strain of dis-pleasure at the thought of the public, popular epitaph that will follow the close of the war. The young poets who survived were more intent on pointing out how the sense of the reality of the war would fade with time, and on trying on the whole to keep it alive, than on producing anything like Binyon's 'For the Fallen'. But what they did do was to celebrate certain aspects of the war while it was taking place, allowing neither bitterness nor hatred to take over. Death was one of these aspects, the soldier was another. In both cases they had too firm a grasp on reality to idealise. They were quite aware of the ordinariness of the common fighter, and that there were millions more like him. They celebrate in fact, the age of the common man, the 'little people grown huge with death',[2]

A digit in the cost
Of the planners.[3]

[1] Alex Comfort, 'Stylites' (*A Wreath for the Living*).
[2] Alun Lewis, 'At a Play' (*Raiders' Dawn*).
[3] John Pudney, 'At the Ceremony' (*Commemorations*).

They realise that these men have been forced to become heroes because they live in a war age —

> Who might have remained, and been
> Cobblers or schoolmasters.[1]

There are very few poems idealising leaders, King, or country. Whereas the Anglo-Saxons sang of their particular heroes until it seemed that the ordinary soldier hardly existed in their ranks, they were so full of 'heafod-men',[2] the Second World War poet celebrates the undistinguished, the twentieth-century fighter who is anonymous unless the poet has a personal recollection of a particular friend. He is the soldier who has been

> Made great by history
> By a trick of the light.[1]

It seems to me that future generations will turn to these poets, not to find out what the war was like, but to discover why it was that men endured as much as they did. Kathleen Raine, writing in *New Road* (1943), said:

Poetry written about the war largely disregards all questions of causes and agents. War is an accident, an enemy to the buds of life. It is not a poet's war. No poet has perhaps expressed what this war does mean to those who live in it, or in spite of it, as completely as has Henry Moore in his shelter drawings, but poets who do write of it, write to the same effect as Moore paints – life lives as best it can, trying to disregard the things that seek to destroy it, humble but persistent in the face of death.

[1] Alex Comfort, 'And all but he departed'.
[2] 'heafod-men (A.S.) – chieftains.

CHAPTER EIGHT

The Communal Sense in
Second World War Poetry

'Under great yellow flags and banners of the ancient
Cold
Began the huge migrations
From some primeval disaster in the heart of Man.
There were great oscillations
Of temperature . . . You knew there had once been
warmth'
(EDITH SITWELL, *The Shadow of Cain*)

'Thank God our time is now when wrong
Comes up to face us everywhere,
Never to leave us till we take
The longest stride of soul men ever took.
Affairs are now soul size.'
(CHRISTOPHER FRY, *A Sleep of Prisoners*)

'Like wartime, he was dull'.
(W. H. AUDEN, *In Time of War*)

IN my Introduction, I mentioned two approaches to war – the 'communal' and the 'individual'. It remains to consider which term would best describe the attitude of the Second World War poets. We have seen how most of the poetry produced records the very personal reactions and desires of the poets. They are not sweeping bardic strains for great occasions. On the other hand the knowledge that 'What's done to me is done to many' is never far from their consciousness. But apart from this large collection of personal lyrics there is also a body of poetry that draws upon the sense of community that war inevitably creates, and which I want to concentrate on in this chapter.

The First World War poet tended to restrict his subject matter to the soldier – the men who march away, the fallen, the dead. Yet the poet's changing attitude depended a great deal on the changing face of the war itself as much as his own individual outlook. The personal lyrics produced by diverse hands add up to a body of verse all tending one way and which may be viewed not as the individual soldier's angle on events but as expressing a communal view of soldiership. Some reviewers were making demands for poetry to fit its time. So Lascelles Abercrombie pointed out in 1915 that battle poems, e.g. Tennyson's 'Revenge', had very seldom been contemporary. He thought that patriotism should be characterised by reticence. The patriotic motive must co-exist with the artist, a point proved by the half-failures of Newbolt's 'The Vigil' and Kipling's 'For all we have and are'.[1]

The Second World War poets faced similar demands,[2] and even if they themselves paid little attention to them, the importance they were conceded in the literature of the time depended a great deal on how far they fulfilled those demands. The very fact that those demands were made shows some kind of a communal spirit, if not permeating the age, at least being searched for by the age to answer the need of the time.

The three quotations at the head of this chapter are completely different statements made on the Second World War by three writers of substantial reputation. The first tells us that war is tragic, the second that war is glorious, and the third that war is dull. All three are attitudes fundamental to the second world conflict, and I would suggest that instead of one invalidating another, they add up to a complexity of response.

Most ages, if interviewed on the subject, would consider themselves tragic. What characterises this one is a sense of supreme communal tragedy here and now. Most

[1] *Quarterly Review,* London, October 1915, 'The War and the Poets'.

[2] See Appendix.

of the great epics have viewed man as an archetype in the then known civilisation. During the period we are dealing with, there were two poems in particular which dealt with the epic subject of the race of man, and dealt with it in terms of epic imagery by going back to the Biblical period following the Creation and linking it up with man in his present-day surroundings. The two poems, Edith Sitwell's 'Shadow of Cain' and Auden's 'In Time of War' are poems nearest to the 'epic' of this age – an inverted epic, for both of them see man in his present state as of unheroic stature, 'the little natures that will make us cry'; both picture a decline in man, not only in his state, but also in his nature, through his own evil and weakness. Both lead up to the crisis of the present time – man could reach no lower point, either of evil or of suffering, than he has now come to. So supremely tragic is our age that the whole world disturbance is pictured by Edith Sitwell as comparable with that before the Flood:

> The gulf that was torn across the world seemed as if the beds of all the Oceans
> Were emptied . . . Naked, and gaping at what once had been the Sun,
> Like the mouth of the Universal Famine
> It stretched its jaws from one end of the Earth to the other.

Here is the magnitude of the tragedy. Auden's 'In Time of War' reflects on the other hand the age's awareness of man's size, of how man is getting smaller and smaller, with nothing to rely on. There are, of course, many contributory factors – the expanding universe, for instance, and the vast new philosophies that are still calling all in doubt.

If we consider any epic previous to this century, we notice that the poet sees man as against nature, i.e. man in his own little world. The poet in his elegiac note at the end of 'Beowulf' sees in the fall of a leader the decline of a race, but his conception of 'nature' does not take in the vastness of the universe as we know it today, nor the decline of a race, the fall of humanity as we have seen it in a period when there are so many material benefits in favour of its survival and advancement. The Beowulf poet portrayed the sad fate of heroic man in a hostile environment, while still being bounded by that environment. Even 'Paradise Lost' which set out to recount the 'fall of Man' used the fixed Ptolemaic system – the whole of man's fall is seen within prescribed bounds, with the everlasting arms beneath. But past epic struggles are nothing compared with the negative emptiness poets see facing modern civilisation. Present enemies are loneliness, fear, and corruption, all coming from within, in what appears a limitless universe without Divine planning or upkeep. No doubt War put spark to the tinder, but the fact remains that time and again war is made the stalking horse for the poet's sense of a disturbed civilisation. Auden declares

> O not ever war can frighten us enough;
> That last attempt to eliminate the Strange
>   By uniting us all in a terror
>   Of something known, even that's a failure
> Which cannot stop us taking our walks alone,
> Scared of the unknown, unconditional dark,
>   Down the avenues of our longing.[1]

Spender points out in *New Writing* that this is a political age: 'That is to say political beliefs and events play a part in the lives of contemporaries which religious and spectacular warnings of the working out of doom amongst the great used to play in the past.'[2] We have seen how the Spanish Civil War poets tried, by dying in an ideal cause, to return to the secure world of old values – the heroic and the just. We have seen also how this developed in part

---

[1] 'New Year Letter' (1941).
[2] *Penguin New Writing*, No. 6 (1941). 'Books and the War'.

from the insecurity that appeared to start with the First World War. As Francis Brett Young has described it in 'The Island', the between-war years were given over to Pleasure, Change, and Speed. The evolvement of the Fascist and Communist states may perhaps be attributed to the need for communal safety in an insecure world as much as earlier civilisations found it expedient to pool their resources and form some kind of community.

A sense of man's place in history has come to the fore during this century, as opposed to the mere dealing with historical subjects. The image of man's decline from Creation onwards is its literary rendering. It is history looked upon from the present and given significance. Another side to it is the feeling that the past – the whole of the past and its futile warring – is very much present, and we are expiating it here and now. In Francis Brett Young's 'The Island' we have a diluted instance in the repetition of English history. In Edwin Muir, as in many of the younger fighter poets, there is a finer sense of actually being caught up in a world's history that is

> The jangling
> Of all the voices of plant and beast and man
> That have not made a harmony
> Since first the great controversy began.[1]

Likewise Alun Lewis in India forgets to describe the hardships endured by soldiers on the march in order to reflect on the men who have passed this way before, and to wonder if their thoughts so many years ago matched his own today.[2]

All this contributes to the picture of the human race, not so much divided into nations as partaking of a communal nature. On the other hand the dangers of community life as the twentieth century has developed it are

[1] 'The Narrow Place' (*The Wheel*, 1943).
[2] 'By the gateway of India, Bombay'.

very apparent. We have seen the satire levelled against it by the 1930 poets in particular. This age is probably unique in its awareness of and attack upon the sheep-like herding together of humanity while at the same time laying great stress upon community life. The poets are never tired of telling us of our responsibility to remain individuals. Louis MacNeice in 1941 wrote of his pleasure at being back in England because:

> The typical Englishman contains, paradoxically, an anarchist; this can be seen from English poetry. Any social revolution which is to suit this country must take account of that anarchist. The notorious defects of the English are at least the defects of a people who respect the individual human being . . . When we come out of the tunnel we must still have faces – not masks.[1]

Alex Comfort is one of the Second World War poets who, as we have noted, not only protests against community folly in following the warmongers into two world wars, but pushes forward the other side to the argument – community power for good or ill. At the same time his satire is directed at the men who cannot think for themselves.

But satire speaks to its age and about its age. The reviewers of Second World War poetry required poets to speak on behalf of and for their age. What emerges along with the tragic view in poets like Auden and Edith Sitwell and Alex Comfort, is, as we have seen, intense bitterness and irony. Their satire differs from that of the First World War in not being levelled by soldiers against civilians, but in being an attack on the state of man generally. It doesn't ask Owen's question What are you going to do about us? but asks instead What are we going to do about the present situation, and in doing so underlines the major difference in outlook between the two wars.

[1] Penguin *New Writing*, No. 5 (1941). 'The Way We Live Now' IV.

When a poet like Edith Sitwell writes of the progress of Man in terms of the evolution of the world in biblical and epic imagery, she is setting the scene for the magnitude of the tragedy. The motions of war have become the physical motions of nature:

> There were great emerald thunders in the air
> In the violent Spring, the thunders of the sap and the
>   blood in the heart.[1]

We are aware that the pterodactyl that fouls its nest has the iron wings of a machine age. But strong irony underlies the use of natural terms – there is the inference that we have not progressed much beyond the prehistoric state, at the same time we have not even retained the decencies of natural feeling – the child is left for the baboon to look after, and the baboon does a better job of it than humanity.[2]

Auden's irony is probably strongest in a volume of poems published as late after the war as 1955 – *The Shield of Achilles*. In the actual poem under that title the satire has disappeared completely in face of the general tragedy involved.

> Out of the air a voice without a face
>   Proved by statistics that some cause was just
> In tones as dry and level as the place:
>   No one was cheered and nothing was discussed;
>   Column by column in a cloud of dust
> They marched away enduring a belief
> Whose logic brought them, somewhere else, to grief.

The atom bomb is not without its mention both from Edith Sitwell and D. J. Enright. The latter in his poem 'Monuments of Hiroshima' captures the strangeness and incomprehensibility of this form of warfare to a world that was seeing it for the first time.

[1] *The Shadow of Cain* (1947).
[2] 'Lullaby' (*Street Songs*, 1942).

How then in view of this conception of our age's tragedy, could a poet write?:

> Thank God our time is now when wrong
> Comes up to face us everywhere.[1]

The answer lies in the necessities of war itself, the fact that men went on fighting and suffering and still preserved their sense of humour. Stephen Spender collected together ordinary human incidents in bomb-shattered London in his book *Citizens in War – and after*, to show the courage and willingness with which people at home faced destruction. The war films of the period pandered to the same need. Churchills famous war speeches, while preserving the serious tragic spirit, were of necessity soul-rousing. Likewise a poem like 'The Island' was intended to celebrate our English race of heroes as much as to bewail our plight. Britain's glory is exalted together with the age that will be remembered for our heroism:

> In all my story there has been no page
> Brighter than this: we have lived in a great age;
> The ancient glory fades not from our name
> And goodly is our Island heritage.

Admittedly we are more likely to find this note in minor writers than major, in writers who looked to or relied on popular approval for their subsistence (hence in drama e.g. Fry's *Sleep of Prisoners*, Priestley's *Desert Highway*) than in poets who are more preoccupied with the tragic sense because they are poets.

On the other hand, one of the demands reviewers made upon poetry was that it should offer consolation to its age. If it was to be a complete reflection of its time it could not leave out the spirit that kept up the proverbial Cockney humour. It had to speak to and for a community that was endeavouring as a community to continue in spite of everything.

[1] Fry, *A Sleep of Prisoners* (1951).

I

It might well be questioned at this point whether this poetry of communal endeavour and hope was not really harking back to the Rupert Brooke tradition:

Now God be thanked Who has matched us with His hour.

But the message to be derived from Second World War poetry is rather different. It is the result, not of standing at the start of a great adventure, but of having experienced great disaster. Edith Sitwell captures its flavour at the end of 'The Shadow of Cain':

> Think! When the
> last clamour of the Bought and Sold
> The agony of Gold
> Is hushed . . . When the last Judas-kiss
> Has died upon the cheek of the Starved Man Christ, these
>   ashes that were Men
> Will rise again
> To be our Fires upon the Judgement Day,
> And yet – who dreamed that Christ has died in vain?
> He walks again on the Seas of Blood, He comes in the
>   terrible Rain.

It is in effect, what reviewers sought, the consolation and healing coming after a straight look at war's destruction. Then the epic heights to which Edith Sitwell raises both disaster and hope in the same breath differs from the ideal heights to which Brooke and Grenfell raised the subject of war. With Edith Sitwell, we might compare Dylan Thomas, 'The Death of a child by Fire', for instance, in which biblical terms raise one child's death into a supreme example of final victory that no sorrow can touch, because

After the first death there is no other.

Such a poem was written to console its readers both by what it says and the way in which it says it. Many poets were drawing upon the Bible for their imagery at this time – we find it in writers as diverse as Dylan Thomas, Edith

Sitwell, George Barker, Christopher Fry, Stephen Spender, and Sidney Keyes. A conscious return in a time of distress reflects a common feature of the war period.

Those writers who did turn their minds to producing a poetry of forgiveness and resolution usually have the maturity of their experience of suffering. Edith Sitwell in particular, both because of her age and her position of onlooker, might be compared with Hardy when he reached the end of the First World War and wrote 'In Time of the Breaking of Nations'. In 'An Old Woman' Edith Sitwell touches on Hardy's theme in her fine paean on how all manner of things shall be well:

> Wise is the earth, consoling grief and glory,
> The golden heroes proud as pomp of waves –
> Great is the earth embracing them, their graves,
> And great is the earth's story.
>
> . . . .
>
> The world's huge fevers burn and shine, turn cold,
> Yet the heavenly bodies and young lovers burn and shine.[1]

These poets are saying, not that there is glory in war, but that glory can come out of war – if we want evidence, then we must look at the way people pull through. Especially do we find among the poets who took part in tasks like the home guard, a sense of consolation arising from their job. What they are doing is not only for their own preservation, but because they are linked to the land and the people they guard. It emerges particularly in Day Lewis and in Edward Shanks. The latter in his 'Night Watch for England' brings to the reader his own immediate awareness of that which he is guarding, in the same way as the younger poets insisted on the beauty of the life they were leaving.

> But I am not alone.
> My outstretched palm rubs on the short rough grass,

[1] 'Street Songs' (1942).

My fingers crush a scabious flower, I can
Prick myself with the gorse or bring the wild thyme
Fragrant from ground to nostril.
All these I love, for these I watch tonight,
For these, and for the village in the valley,
And my own house in it.

The sense of tradition – of English tradition – is part of this feeling for the value of our common heritage, although it is usually the older generation who record it.

The awareness of what is valuable in the life around them was probably there by contrast with the destructive and sordid elements of war. Demetrios Capetanakis saw the writers of the '30s in a similar position. Taking Spender's 'O young men, oh young comrades' as an example, he wrote: 'Such dreams of a beautiful, luminous and joyful humanity were only one of the ways by which the pre-occupation of the poets with the ugliness, greyness and misery oppressing and deadening man, was expressed.'[1]

We have noticed that in both the Spanish Civil War and the Second World War, many poets were preoccupied with the depths to which humanity as a whole can (even willingly) descend. Admittedly Spender in *New Writing and Daylight* (1941) writes: 'Today it is so difficult to be a poet of the public virtues, the public suffering, the public shame, the public aspirations, and the public glory, that many people deny that it is possible.' But he seems to refer more to speaking openly and officially on behalf of a nation and as part of the nation than to writing poetry to answer the common need of the time. The poets accomplished the latter by reference not to nations so much as to themselves – and themselves as part of a suffering community. The 'I', except in a very objective poet like Edith Sitwell, is omnipresent, though in the background. In

[1] *New Writing and Daylight*, Summer 1943: 'Notes on some contemporary writers.'

poems dealing with or aware of the war, the 'I' very rarely remains in a vacuum. Spender's 'Returning to Vienna 1947'[1] is an example of how the poet as a person is affected by the destruction of those things he has valued personally, yet the courage shining from the ruins themselves, the community endurance typified by Vienna puts to shame the selfishness of individual loss:

> I lacked
> That which makes cities not to fall
> The drop of agonising sweat which changes
> Into impenetrable crystal upon crosses
> Which bear cathedrals.

There is a continual intertwining of the communal sense with the individual in Second World War poetry. In discussing himself the poet is dealing with matters that are the concern of a whole community, even though that concern may be momentary only.

The third fundamental communal response to the war was summed up in Auden's description of the Unknown Soldier:

> Like wartime, he was dull.

On the whole, we might say that community nature makes for dullness – but especially during the last war. Compare, for instance, the English uniforms of the Second World War, with those of any major conflict before 1914. The nineteenth-century red and gold was at least labelled by Gilbert as 'South Kensington', but present-day army cloth is surely nearer to 'Shoreditch'. So much of it was technical and incomprehensible warfare, so much depended on not being seen, on not showing one's colours, on finding one's way through colourless food and blinded streets. But apart from that, life was built up on utilitarian principles – transportable, collapsible, bulky and durable –

[1] *The Edge of Being* (1949).

red-brick air-raid shelters and rubber gas-masks – a
cardboard war whose exhibits look shoddy when placed
side by side with the artistic products of previous generations.

Possibly too, in a period of boredom and neurosis, the
common tragedy of the age was that even war was dull.
Rupert Brooke had looked to it as an opportunity to get
away from the stagnation of peace, to rouse history once
again. But he made no reference to the day-to-day realities
of war. In *Homage to Catalonia* George Orwell tells us of
the lice that infested the Spanish trenches and points out
that soldiers all down the ages must have been troubled by
them. But it is in this century that they have been brought
to the notice of the public. That is one reason why war is
no longer 'rattling good history'. Because men have discussed it without reference to honour, glory and patriotism, what war is like both in the abstract, and as an experience with the dignity discarded. Consider the following
lines written by Julian Bell before the outbreak of the
Second World War:

> War is a game for the whole mind,
> An art of will and eye,
> No brothering of mankind
> Or hating inconstantly:
> A hard art of foreseeing,
> Of not too much caring.[1]

What has gone out of war since Brooke and Grenfell's
time is the note of excitement, and what is substituted is 'a
hard art of foreseeing'. In other words, the finer emotions
which are traditionally associated with military heroism
are played down, and the emphasis is laid instead on the
necessity for the blunting of other, equally fine feelings:

> No brothering of mankind
> Or hating inconstantly.

[1] 'Vienna' (*Work for the Winter*, 1936).

Finally there is one element lacking in English war poetry that can be found in the French, and which probably gives to the latter a sense of a whole community completely at one in its suffering which nothing else can give to the former to any comparable degree. It is the poetry of defeat with its overpowering sadness and helplessness, its looking back upon the things that have passed, its traditional roses and lilies in a poet like Aragon, that expressed the strongest bond. The English poet, Alex Comfort, in his poem 'France'[1] captures something of the feeling of a whole country being swept by one wind, and Patric Dickinson in his imaginative and symbolic conception of England as an Occupied Country in *Stone in the Midst* portrays the strength of individual freedom in its inherent inability to accept inevitable oppression. It binds more than the present members of a household together – it is

> One tune, one marching song –
> And your lives are my words
> The dead one, my brother,
> The unborn, his child.

But English poets on the whole could not realise (nor in their position dared they realise) the strains of actual defeat. In any case they would not have had the background that France had in her series of occupations. The dominant English note is that of eventual triumph.

[1] *A Wreath for the Living.*

APPENDIX

Reviewers on the Poetry

IT may be of some interest to consider contemporary reactions to the poets' reflections on war and what sort of encouragement or discouragement poets who published their reflections received. For this purpose I have examined opinion expressed mainly in three reviews – the *Spectator*, the *New Statesman*, and the *Listener*, in order to capture if not the thoughts of the general reader of poetry at least what the general reader of poetry was expected to think, and what the general reader of poetry might demand from the poets themselves. I have occasionally supplemented this census of opinion by looking at various other critical reviews that seemed worth noting.

Today's reader who has gone through the twentieth-century revulsion against the sanctity of organised destruction is likely to be astounded at what was being written during the First World War. Nowhere is there a clearer indication of the divorce that came to exist between England at home and the soldier abroad. The publication in the *Spectator* quite early in the war, of a so-far unpublished poem by Tennyson under the label 'This poem seems almost as if it were written for the present crisis', was indicative of much poetry and much reviewing that was to follow. A few lines from one verse will indicate both quality and sentiments:

> Nine hundred thousand slaves in arms
>   May seek to bring us under;
> But England lives, and still will live,
>   For we'll crush the despot yonder.

> Are we ready, Britons all?
> To answer foes with thunder?
> Arm, arm, arm![1]

The qualities that the *Spectator* reviewer obviously wished to see in a poem were either recruiting ones or ones that justified the soldier's task and even the soldier's death. The appeal to popular sentiment tended to limelight those very qualities we now associate disparagingly with Georgian poetry. The *Spectator* in a very typical review of 1916 admits that it gives, as it feels rightly, priority to those poets who have laid down their lives:

> The memorial volume of letters and poems by the late Captain Colwyn Philipps reveals, among other engaging traits, his passionate attachment to his Welsh home, his touching devotion to his mother – 'the pilot of my soul', as he calls her in the beautiful verses which stand first of all – his love of horse and beast and bird, and his simple, wholesome outdoor philosophy. Captain Philipps's catholic taste is shown by the delightful tribute to 'R.K.' and the admiration for Browning expressed in his letters. Altogether, this is a worthy record of a gallant soldier whose heroic end crowned and fulfilled the ideals expressed in his verse.[2]

The recruiting qualities of the reviews themselves are strongly evident as part of the national duty of a reviewer of English poetry in a time of strife, in the following specimen:

> All lovers of good verse joined to high courage, the joy of battle, and the fighting spirit in its happiest and most exalted mood will delight in Mr. Herbert Asquith's 'The Volunteer and other poems'. . . . There is something always extraordinarily attractive in the combination of

[1] The *Spectator*, October 3rd, 1914.
[2] The *Spectator*, May 27th, 1916.

the scholar and the soldier, as Shakespeare made us understand in 'Hamlet'.[1]

This volume does introduce poems of actual warfare, and the *Spectator* goes so far as to admit their importance, but even so it isn't giving up without a struggle to retain in the reader the correct sense of proportion: 'Though these poems of actual battle are what render the volume so memorable, many readers will no doubt be charmed with the little poem, "To a Baby Found Paddling near the Lines".'

Robert Graves who reached the trenches before Siegfried Sassoon has recorded his meeting with that young poet and tells how the realistic detail he was including in his verse was criticised by Sassoon because 'war should not be written about in a realistic way'. It wasn't long of course before Sassoon himself, having partaken of the realities of war, expressed them far more outrageously than Graves was ever prone to do, but the remark was typical of an attitude that persisted among reviewers and most strongly in the *Spectator* reviews. When it came to look at Robert Graves's volume from the front, *Over the Brazier*, its praise of poetic merit was mingled with excuses, for its readers' benefit, for the poet's views on account of youth. It said of the poems:

> Though in many ways they conform to the new fashion of literary attack, soon to grow old and conventional, they have a touch of true originality, both in the style and in the thoughts underlying the style. Mr. Graves is one of those lucky poets who are able to see and describe things with a difference. His poems (if he will pardon us for saying anything so appallingly commonplace) have all the faults of youth, but they have also a great many of its virtues. He overstrains the note constantly, but, lucky poet ! this does not matter in 1916.[2]

[1] The *Spectator*, January 1st, 1916.
[2] The *Spectator*, June 16th, 1916.

The *New Statesman* was much less prone than the *Spectator* to review contemporary war poetry. It had a more refined conscience where merit was concerned and admitted the ephemeral nature of much that was being written and published. When it did succumb to the fashion, as in its review on some of Siegfried Sassoon's poetry, it tended to have the same cautious approach to the iconoclastic: 'Mr. Sassoon's bent is not so easy to detect; his work is clouded with the horrors of war, and neither loathing of these nor destestation of the smug civilians who cheerfully accept them is likely to produce durable poetry.'[1] The new volume of *Georgian Poetry 1916–17*, which introduced nine new poets to the public, was reviewed for the *New Statesman* by Edward Shanks, who tended to play down the importance of the horrific:

> On a first reading, the book communicates a distinct impression of battle, murder and sudden death. . . . But a closer examination reveals the fact that this impression is derived almost wholly from Mr. Sassoon, Mr. Nichols and Mr. Graves, and does not give a complete or a correct notion even of them. The military inspiration in the book, apart from the very special emphasis put upon it by these three writers, is really very slight; and there is nothing to prove that the war has yet had any serious effect on the development of English poetry.[2]

In a short notice towards the end of the war the *New Statesman* reviews *Poems written during the Great War 1914–18* and while admitting that it is wholesome to have a counterblast to war idealism, still boggles at the too blatant expression of some of the evils of war. The book, it says, gives the impression that only evil forces are

[1] *New Statesman*, November 24th, 1917.
[2] *New Statesman*, December 22nd, 1917.

involved and 'this is a false and harmful doctrine to spread abroad'.[1]

The *Spectator* a month later gives vent to its own revulsion from the sort of poetry that by this time was flowing fairly freely from the trenches. The reviewer is quite taken aback at the *saeva indignatio* expressed in Alec Waugh's volume, *Resentment*: 'He dwells almost exclusively on the ugliness, dirt, and physical horrors of war, on the plight of the unburied dead, on discontent and doubts and fears.'[2]

When Wilfred Owen's work was published in 1920 no reviewer could ignore either the poetic power or the message. The *Spectator* cites Owen's human sympathy, and the *New Statesman* hints at what has made other 'realist' poets before Owen fail where it must be admitted he succeeds. The reviewer quotes Owen's introduction that he is concerned with the pity of war, not with poetry, and comments: 'It is strange that this avowal should have come from one of the few war-poets of this type, whose work never once has about it the false ring of mere propaganda.'[3] Other poets (e.g. Sassoon) the review goes on, present merely intellectual concepts where Owen has arrested the imagination as soon as the intellect.

It is obvious from these First World War reviews that the soldier-poet and the home-reader were not by the end of the war together in their view of what poetry could and should accomplish in a time of crisis. As Graves has pointed out, most First World War poetry came into existence for the very reason that men in the fighting line felt that civilians were out of touch. That the points these poets were making came home to stay can be seen from the fact that reviewers of the 'thirties were frequently demanding from the poet exactly what he was producing,

[1] *New Statesman*, September 21st, 1918.

[2] *Spectator*, October 12th, 1918.

[3] *New Statesmen*, January 15th, 1921.

namely comment on the political, social, and military scene. During the Second World War the demands of reviewers were as we shall see rather different.

We must keep in mind with regard to the various magazines and reviews their political preferences, for example the *New Statesman* inclined to the Left, the *Spectator* rather more to the Right. During the First World War the *Spectator*'s rather traditional, patriotic approach to the situation emerges quite obviously, I think, in its comments on the poetry being produced. As we come on to the 'thirties, we must also keep in mind that many reviews were written by the poets themselves or by writers with decided political leanings, with the result that if a review is not downright biased, it is sometimes coloured. (Spender's review of Campbell's *Flowering Rifle* is one of the best examples of this.)

The reviews of the 'thirties are indicative of a different political climate from our own. The fact that the New Movement, as it was called, was Communist in politics was mentioned and accepted without the comment it would arouse today. Critics were inclined to label all the major poets of the movement as belonging to the Communist Party. No absolute sympathy is expressed by reviewers (outside definitely partisan critics belonging to the Left magazines), but on the other hand there is not a shade of antagonism. One critic actually makes the statement on *Trial of a Judge* that

in his thinking Mr. Spender is scrupulously fair.[1]

Moreover, the new vitality embodied in the movement, it was suggested, was a sign of the recovery of the age itself in the social-political sphere. As a result: 'The second anthology of "new signatures", *New Country*, was noticeably more Communistic than the first, and rich in what

[1] *The Spectator*, March 18th, 1938. Nevill Coghill.

Mr. Lewis calls "adventitious energy".' The very fact
that the poets had come together in a movement was beginning to arouse public interest in them (even though
they had published separately before then).[1]

The *Criterion* was one magazine which, while admitting that it was not entirely in sympathy with the views
expressed in *New Writing*, at least agreed that it embodied
many present-day feelings and should be admired for
taking a stand and doing something about them:

> This change, then, in the significance of the word 'new'
> shows the increasing anxiety among writers, as well as
> everyone else, to find something firm to cling to in the
> apparent chaos of contemporary life; the determination
> to be on one side or other of the fence, not sitting on it as
> a mark for both parties.[2]

Yet the main complaint against the 1930 poets lies in
the group heritage. It is their common fund of opinions
and images that critics proclaim a hindrance to their individual development:

> leaving the ground, we sit in tethered balloons, the spec-
> tators of a mimic warfare, while round us the kestrel
> (sole bird of this new world) swoops, and the bully-boys
> of the Muse romp among the clouds like porpoises.
> There are few occasions when this scene, or part of it, is
> not invoked. It is the New Country. . . . That is the
> mechanical and bad side of the group product.[3]

The good side, the review goes on, lies in their genuine
futurism, for in seeing present society as doomed the poets
have a new vision.

Day Lewis and Spender are continually blamed for not

[1] *New Statesman*. October 27th, 1934. G. W. Stonier reviewing
the third edition of *New Signatures*.

[2] Vol. XVI 1936–7 Frank Chapman reviewing *New Writing*.

[3] *New Statesman*, March 9th, 1935. G. W. Stonier reviewing *A
Time to Dance, Collected Poems*.

integrating politics and poetry.[1] The political and literary groove of the 1930s, apart from its initial newness, is seen rather as something each poet has to step out of before his individual genius can emerge. Spender is seen as a personal poet even in the midst of politics, and the incongruity is noted.[2] And Day Lewis, we are told, fails when his poetry is determined by purpose rather than by feeling.[3] Even in the 1940s, his faults are laid at the door of the previous decade:

> One of the best poets of the '30s, Mr. Day Lewis is still, to some extent, mesmerised by the ideas and phraseology of the period, but in poems like 'The Poet' and 'Reconciliation' there is a freedom and spontaneity which promises new development.[4]

The critics themselves were, at the beginning of the 1930s, intrigued by a poetry that spoke directly to the age. By the time the Second World War came, they were urging the immediate need for something to be said on the world's plight. (In fact it is amazing how up-to-date poets were expected to be. In reviewing MacNeice's *The Last Ditch* and Hamilton's *The Sober War* the *Listener* remarks: 'neither . . . shows any prophetic awareness, in these poems written some months ago, of the summer of Blitzkrieg.'[5]

Although there was no explicit demand for contemporaneity at the beginning of the 'thirties, in a review of *Noah and the Waters*, in the middle of the decade, we are told to remember that whatever its faults it has a

[1] *Spectator*, November 9th, 1934. I. M. Parsons reviewing *Vienna*.

[2] *New Statesman*, October 27th, 1934. G. W. Stonier reviewing Spender's *Poems*.

[3] *Spectator*, March 22nd, 1935. Edwin Muir.

[4] *Spectator*, March 3rd 1944. S. Shannon reviewing *Word over all*.

[5] *Listener*, August 15th, 1940.

contemporary value, that Day Lewis can be read with interest even when he is writing badly, whereas Church, Palmer, and W. J. Turner are enjoyable only when they write well.[1]

The Ascent of F6 is praised for being 'a topical morality' – 'the self immolation of a good individual in the service of capitalism.'[2] *Trial of a Judge* is hailed as a modern tragedy: 'Considered as a fable then this play is of gripping interest in a world which has just witnessed the wolfish invasions of Austria and the threat of ballot by bullet.'[3] There is no doubt that though many older writers, favourites like Blunden and Housman, were still being published at this time, it was the Auden group that was in fashion. When Blunden's *Elegy and other poems* came upon the market in 1938, the reviewer sought to put him forward by denying the charge of escapist, he at least expressed the 'spiritual disillusionment' where more fashionable poets reflected political and social poverty.

The age itself is at times very much aware of its own nature. In reviewing 'Spain' (Auden), 'War-Dance' (Graham-Howe), and 'Epic of the Alcazar' (Major Geoffrey Mosse), Connolly in the *New Statesman* points out the link between these three completely different writers, i.e. they are obsessed by war, fighting, and death, because the age itself is one of sensation hunters who desire strong meat: 'They are people who have grown up on crises, for whom bad news is better than no news, victims of the war fever which is on the increase twenty years after 1914, which may be universal in thirty.' But, as he remarks on the Spanish Civil War – 'no one seems able

[1] *New Statesman*, April 4th, 1936. G. W. Stonier.

[2] *cf.* July 1940, T. C. Worsley reviewing *Another Time*: 'Reading Auden, even at his most obscure or his most silly, enlarges our understanding of what the life of our day is really like.'

[3] *Spectator*, March 18th, 1938. Nevill Coghill.

to stop.'[1] Critics, in fact, are not inclined to accept even
fine poetry if the note it strikes is a false one. Day Lewis,
for instance, is criticised for his lines 'Tell them in England . . .' This is too much like Brooke and Flecker, and
their period, the reviewer knows, is over. The age has its
equivalent only in Roy Campbell.[2]

The fact that the 1930 poets were intent on speaking to
and for their age, then, was not objected to. Their efforts
and the poetry they produced in the Spanish Civil War
was reviewed with considerable sympathy. What was
objected to was the manner in which they chose to reflect
the age. For one thing it was limited in appeal. Auden is
praised for the width of view his poetry can give, the sheer
physical outlook, the continents and races he surveys from
vast heights.[3] The other poets have more limited capabili-
ties though within their limitations some of them are still
valued as highly as Auden. But the limitation of the group
as a whole lies in the emphasis on the intellectual and
cerebral at the expense of the emotional and sensuous.
Another Time is criticised for the poverty of its verse and
the way in which it derides the heroic and romantic.[4]
Even as early as 1934, the *Listener* was writing:

> It was evident in Mr. Pudney's first book of poems,
> *Spring Encounter*, that here was a poet in whom the
> social sense, though keenly developed, was not going to
> be exploited at the expense of that sensuous appeal
> which is the basis of all true poetry.

Except for Spender who embodies some of the 'true
poetry', other writers are simply protracting Eliot's 'Waste
Land'.[5]

[1] *New Statesman*, June 5th, 1937. Cyril Connolly.
[2] *New Statesman*, December, 3rd, 1938. G. W. Stonier.
[3] *Spectator*, December 4th, 1936. Edwin Muir reviewing 'Look
Stranger'.
[4] *Listener*, August 22nd, 1940.
[5] *Listener*, October 31st, 1934.

K

Then there is the further criticism of obscurity. The *Criterion*, which may be taken as one of the most liberal-minded reviews of the period, while accepting much of Auden's work as praiseworthy though admitting it difficult to understand, still has to give up Rex Warner's *Poems* as a bad job : 'his revolutionary verse is so drenched in the mysticism of violence and so remote from political realities that one does not know what to make of it.'[1]

Another aspect of the same problem was the reliance on fact at the expense of artistic integrity. The *Criterion* points out how much style is sacrificed to politics in *New Writing*.[2] The *Listener* reviewing the new series that started in 1939 quoted:

> 'I saw clumsy Life again at her stupid work' – Henry James's remark . . . would shock most of the contributors to New Writing. In nearly all the stories, descriptions and poems included here, truth to the fact, to what actually happened, is the chief consideration . . . The authors show us how human beings behave in the shadow of war, fascism and unemployment; but they do not follow any one formula.[3]

The second major complaint after that of limitation was that the 1930 style of writing dated. Even in the 1930s. As early as 1937 Rex Warner's *Poems* elicited the comment 'Mr. Warner combines a love of birds with an already old-fashioned habit of hailing the Red Dawn.'[4] So much for the political ideals – the style of writing received stronger criticism because it outlasted even those ideals. As Spender observed, the left-wing orthodox party gradually grew into a genre which writers followed

---

[1] Vol. XVII 1937–8. Edwin Muir reviewing Warner's *Poems*.
[2] Vol. XVI 1936–7. Frank Chapman reviewing *New Writing*.
[3] *Listener*, June 1st, 1939. 'New Writings: New Series No. 2.'
[4] *Spectator*, June 4th, 1937.

willy-nilly.[1] Rook, for instance, was reprimanded for writing in a facile manner that had much of the older writers about it.[2]

Both the style of writing and of thinking was out-dated by the time the Second World War broke out. The *Listener* preferred those poems of Lehmann written prior to 1934 and after 1939, because the between years were full of clichés.[3] And looking back in 1941 on a period of which she had been part, Rosamund Lehmann remarks: 'Far away that time seems now, with its feverish anti-Fascist slogans and frivolous pro-freedom gestures; the dilemma of

> Whether to die
> Or live within fear's eye.'[4]

In his 1936 Postscript to *A Hope for Poetry* C. Day Lewis sees both a revival of interest in poetry and

> a reaction from the recent pre-occupation of poets with social justice, their possibly over-mechanised vocabulary, and often slapdash technique: a return to the ideals of poetic integrity and artistic individualism: a setting-out-again in the direction of 'pure' poetry.

The new school of Surrealist poets that appeared with *the white horseman* was quick to seize upon the changing trend of the age to boost their own brand of writing. In the Introduction G. S. Fraser pointed out that

> Nobody denies the immediate social impact of much of the poetry of Auden, Spender, or MacNeice. But it was, to a certain extent, an impact of the surface and of the

[1] *New Statesman*, December 9th, 1939. Spender: 'Old Wine in New Bottles!.

[2] *Listener*, September 10th, 1942. *Poems of this war.*

[3] December 31st, 1942. Lehmann's *Forty Poems.*

[4] *New Statesman*, March 29th, 1941. Rosamund Lehmann reviewing Day Lewis' *Poems in Wartime* and *Selected Poems.*

moment. The war, as a matter of fact, has made that sort of immediate political approach, that clear-cut partisanship, a practical impossibility. But, to have social value, poetry does not have to show immediate political relevance.

The major poets were quicker at heeding the warning of reviewers than their followers. MacNeice was praised in 1945 for moving with the times,[1] and Day Lewis for freeing himself from his early politics.[2] In the meantime the style that younger writers followed was associated especially with the names of Auden and Spender. Gascoyne is found guilty once of descending to the bathos of the '40's which was worthy of Spauden.[3]

The third great complaint against the 1930 poets is that they stood essentially for a certain class at a certain time. *The Still Centre* was unsatisfactory because the poems are documents 'not of "the human situation" in general, but only of the situation of many English intellectuals today'.[4] The movement that was accepted at the opening of the 1930s, after the disappointment of its early hopes, came to a sudden standstill.[5] The actual fight against fascism in the Second World War was not seen, even by the writers themselves, as the glorious outcome of their warnings in the '30s. The New Movement was merely a pointer to the times and not one that went any further. It was discovered that the movement did not move – partly because the remedy it proposed was palpably ineffective, partly be-

[1] *Listener*, March 29th, 1945. *Springboard*.

[2] *Listener*, October 13th, 1938. Edwin Muir reviewing *Overtures to Death*.

[3] *New Statesman*, January 22nd, 1944. G. W. Stonier reviewing Gascoyne's *Poems 1937–42*.

[4] *Listener*, May 18th, 1939. F. T. Prince reviewing *The Still Centre* (supplement).

[5] *Spectator*, July 26th, 1940. M. Roberts reviewing *Another Time* –'gives the impression that Mr. Auden used up all his energy in treating the Spanish Civil War as a crusade.'

cause its crisis had come in the Spanish Civil War, and with disillusionment came the abandonment of all hope. Elizabeth Bowen notices that in Lehmann's account of *New Writing in Europe*, he 'writes of the Spanish war with a capital W and of the present war with a small one,' that the poets he deals with

> became 'intellectuals' – it is notable that Mr. Lehmann identifies intellectuals with writers – and, by grouping, located themselves, whether abroad or in England, inside the intellectuals' world: isolated, special, intensive, charged with personal feeling and, in the long run, as claustrophobic as any middle-class home. Would it be unfair to say of this group of writers, that, though they changed their milieu, they never fully emerged, but remained life's delicate children after all?[1]

Critics had been pleased to find poets like Auden and Spender reflecting the 'fascist trauma' in their drama. But as time went on there were fresh aspects of a new age that they demanded should be dealt with. And the 1930 poets, in abandoning their political principles, were rather inclined to retire into a private world. MacNeice for instance, exhibited during the war a 'sickening atmosphere of self-pity', and his 'chief feeling seems to be one of quite natural, though not very significant annoyance at its interfering with his rather complex personal life.'[2]

For, although critics were wanting a new outlook on the world, they still wanted an awareness of that world and its significance in our time to be at the centre of the poet's outlook. Kathleen Raine summed up the situation during the Second World War:

[1] *Spectator*, January 17th, 1941. Elizabeth Bowen reviewing *New Writing in Europe*.

[2] *Listener*, August 15th, 1940, reviewing MacNeice's *The Last Ditch*.

The poets of the last generation – Auden, MacNeice, Empson, Michael Roberts, Day Lewis, Robert Graves, have one great merit that the younger poets on the whole lack. That is, an adult and responsible attitude towards society. Readers of Poetry London, that most representative selection from the poetry being written now, will be aware that in the tendency to return to 'pure' poetry there has been a corresponding weakening of the poets' grasp of history in progress. The same turning away from the world is expressed in a great deal of current erotic poetry. Not because it is erotic, but because sex has become for the moment the expression of the individual who can't cope with society in larger units.[1]

There were, of course, still people like Read whose *World within a War* was political in the '30s manner and therefore out-of-date; his war poetry is 'an accomplished but minor comment on a human situation that has left him behind.'[2] The older generation of writers are the ones who are usually blamed for having little of significance to say during the war even when they are writing on it. Hamilton's anti-German poetry belongs to a different age. Nineteen thirty-nine required something different, not militancy but healing: 'One cannot look to Mr. Hamilton for that terrible awareness of contemporary life which – if one could accept it – might indeed find a way to console us.'[3]

The middle generation, when they do have something to say, are greatly appreciated. And what they are especially praised for is thinking in tune with their time. MacNeice in *The Earth Compels*, writes of the usual worries and delights of life, but

[1] *New Road* (1943). 'Are poets doing their duty?'

[2] *Listener*, September 16th, 1944. H. Read's *World within a War*.

[3] *Listener*, August 15th, 1940. G. Rostrevor Hamilton's *The Sober War*.

What is more important than all this, is that the poet is afraid. He is haunted by the fears that have been haunting us all – fears of war, the future, regimentation, the unknown – and it looks as if these fears are the making of him as a poet.[1]

On the other hand, it is fully recognised that MacNeice and his group are writing a war-time poetry rather than war poetry. Their value lies in writing 'the news behind the news', i.e. they extract truth from the experience of war.[2] And the poetry that is usually accepted as reflecting its age is more often than not characterised by 'the virtues of seriousness and humility'. This it is that Pudney lacks and which Church's *Twentieth Century Psalter* possesses.[3] Edith Sitwell, we are told, is at her best during the war and writing more selflessly because of it.[4] MacNeice's *Plant and Phantom* is praised for not overstating, and 'That, in these days, is something of an achievement.'[5] Kathleen Raine objects to the aggressive approach of W. R. Rogers – 'for experience is inviolable and remains a still, small voice, very unlike Mr. Rogers's histrionic shout.'[6]

Besides these, critics require from the poets maturity, humanity, and the correct sense of values. What had to be taken into account was the change in outlook that war

[1] *Spectator*, June 10th, 1938. W. Plomer reviewing *The Earth compels*.

[2] *New Statesman*, January 27th, 1945. Brian Howard reviewing *Springboard* and Barker's *Eros in Dogma*.

[3] *New Statesman*, April 17th, 1943. Spender reviewing *Twentieth Century Psalter*.

[4] *New Statesman*, April 4th, 1942. Spender reviewing *Street songs*.

[5] *New Statesman*, May 10th, 1941. G. W. Stonier reviewing *Plant and Phantom*.

[6] *Spectator*, October 31st, 1941. Kathleen Raine reviewing *Awake* (W. R. Rogers).

brought about. We have already noted the suffering im-
plicit in the work of the middle generation of writers. It
was the human touch that was appreciated more than
anything by reviewers. Day Lewis's home guard poems for
instance had a special mention.[1] Kathleen Raine points
out that A. L. Rowse's work shows the changing influences of the age, beginning with the *Homo Rationalis* and
his hatred for various natural forms of life – e.g. lovers,
and the mother suckling her child. But

> was war the angel that so absolutely reversed Mr.
> Rowse's values? (And not, I repeat, his alone, for we
> were all in it.) Certain only that the conversion came,
> and it is with the same intelligence that the *Homo
> Rationalis* writes in 1940 with so much tenderness for
> an anonymous soldier.[2]

Perhaps it is because of the 'human' appeal of their
work that women writers come off so well in reviews. The
maturity of poetesses like Edith Sitwell and Kathleen
Raine is constantly emphasised.[3] They have digested the
experiences of war and reformulated life.

The war greatly affected the critics' outlook on poetry,
just as much as it affected the poets' outlook on life. Poetry
was praised when it answered the need of the time.
Hence:

> The experience of the last two years has helped us to
> find more in Eliot and Auden than we saw at first, but it
> has shown up the shallowness of Roy Campbell's cocky
> poems.[4]

Personal bitterness in Graves is condemned, along with

---

[1] *Listener*, January 9th, 1941. Day Lewis's *Poems in Wartime*.

[2] *Spectator*, October 31st, 1941. Kathleen Raine reviewing
Poems of a Decade (A. L. Rowse).

[3] *Listener*, March 19th, 1942. *Street Songs, Stone and Flower
1938–43*.

[4] *Spectator*, March 28th, 1946. Janet Adam Smith reviewing
Sons of the Mistral (Campbell).

self-pity and resentment in Spender.[1] And the age itself is aware both of the poet's problem and of its own. The former is how much the poet should 'give himself to the present and how much must he stand aside in order to retain an essential measure of detachment.'[2] The latter is the choice the age must exercise to fulfil its own need.

> Today a writer in the traditional forms of poetry is unlikely to obtain his due measure of praise, for we are living in a time when content is divorced from form, and when mere topicality of subject-matter is decisive in winning contemporary attention – just as it may make most of the work of our contemporary writers unreadable in days to come.[3]

The number of lyrics produced during the war was put down both to the way war detaches a writer from his cultural community (therefore he turns to personal experience),[4] and also to the need of the age for lyric poetry 'to resolve in the individual soul the conflict of emotions aroused by the experience of living and loving in a threatened world.'[5]

The Introduction to *the white horseman* sought to excuse what might appear 'escapist' poetry by asking the reader to

> consider what world we are living in. With the war, we are all forced in a sense to become stoics – to depend on ourselves and the universe, the intermediate social worlds having been largely destroyed . . . It is only natural, really, that a certain quality of gloom, loneliness, excess, should strike the ordinary reader, about the poetry of our generation.

[1, 2] *Spectator*, May 8th, 1942. S. Shannon.

[3] *Spectator*, May 8th, 1942. Review of *The Hope of Dawn and other poems* (Edwyn Bevan).

[4] *Listener*, March 18th, 1943.

[5] *Spectator*, February 3rd, 1939. John Hayward reviewing *The Year's Poetry 1938*.

The emergence of the younger generation of writers in some respects fulfilled and in others failed to fulfil the demands of the critics. For one thing the glut of poems that went into anthologies like *Poems from the Forces* might reflect the age, but certainly was not representative of the best achievement of the age. The poets had not had enough time to reach maturity either of life or of work. And as one reviewer remarked 'one poem does not make a poet'. Some writers were too derivative both in style and emotion, and most would probably cease writing altogether at the end of the war. Compared with *Poems for Spain*, *Poems from the Forces* lacks spontaneity and is at times embarrassing.[1] Another criticism of young writers is that they 'write poems as the result of their education',[2] and again they do not think – 'they are merely tormented, bewildered, flummoxed by thought.'[3]

But the new movement recognised among the young poets is praised on the whole. Another review of *Poems from the Forces* takes a wider view of the issue and counts most interesting those who are writing from inexperience.[4] Individual poets are praised for directness, for truth, for ordinary human feeling, and for reflecting the emotions and thoughts of their own generation. It is observed that 'most poets who deal with the war contemplate, not the war itself, but themselves as affected by it'.[5] This came to be accepted as a necessity at first. As time wore on, however, it became symptomatic of an age when distinctions were disappearing and war and its

[1] *Listener*, February 12th, 1942.

[2] *Spectator*, January 8th, 1943. S. Shannon.

[3] *New Statesman*, January 31st, 1942. Edwin Muir reviewing Church's *The Solitary Man*.

[4] *New Statesman*, March 28th, 1942. G. W. Stonier reviewing *Poems from the Forces*.

[5] *Listener*, September 10th, 1942. *Poetry in Wartime*. (Tambimuttu).

personal associations became the stock in trade for all poets :

> The distinction between public verse and personal verse may seem to have disappeared. No commemorative ode from the Poet Laureate greets the Moscow Conference, and every soldier who writes a sonnet to his girl asks more or less what we're fighting for.[1]

There is a complaint that all poets must drag in war, whatever they are writing about,[2] yet on the other hand they are praised when they express any part of the thought and feeling of the age – Fuller's sense of exile in time and space for instance,[3] and Keyes's dwelling upon death and self-sacrifice.[4]

Spender, with his usual sensitivity to distinctions, pointed out in *Poetry since 1939* an aspect of our war poetry due to our position as opposed to the position of any country on the Continent. He tells us that we have learnt from the war community responsibility:

> However, the values of imagination which cannot be related to public action, human personality considered apart from civic consciousness, beauty, romantic love, have suffered the neglect which is inevitable in a completely mobilised and conscripted community.

The situation on the continent has been the very opposite :

> The leaders of the Resistance Movements . . . had leisure . . . to learn the human lessons and the poetic values of their experiences.

[1] *New Statesman*, November 6th, 1943. G. W. Stonier reviewing *World Over All*.

[2] *New Statesman*, July 31st, 1943. G. W. Stonier.

[3] *New Statesman*, September 2nd 1944. G. W. Stonier reviewing *A Lost Season*.

[4] *New Statesman*, August 11th, 1945. G. W. Stonier reviewing Keyes' *Collected Poems*.

In such war poetry as England has produced, the intellectual acceptance of a necessary unity on the plane of material action is altogether different from the unity at a personal as well as an ardently patriotic level which we find in the French, the Czech, the Greek, the Norwegian, poetry of Resistance.

Still the communal binding power of much poetry is pointed to by many reviewers as having the healing properties desired by the British public. What is liked particularly in Lehmann's poems is 'the visionary poetry which is a generally shared experience in this explosive today'.[1] What is liked in Richard Church's is

> the constancy of fertile earth shining into branch and bud as antidote to these calamities.[2]

Richard Spender is praised for

> the innocence of a singer, for whom the abstractions of politicians and moralists are of no concern.[3]

Keyes and Alun Lewis receive considerable support for their poems which show a fundamental resemblance in being on 'the single poetic theme of Life and Death'.[4] And to sum up, when Scarfe criticised Prokosch for failing to write poetry 'bearing directly on social matters', the reviewer replied in 1942:

> what poet has or could or would want to? Indirectly, yes – because all great poets are essentially and inevitably of their age – but directly only if they are the

---

[1] *New Statesman*, April 17th, 1943. Spender reviewing Lehmann's *Forty Poems*.

[2] *Listener*, April 29th, 1943. *Twentieth Century Psalter*.

[3] *Listener*, May 10th 1945. Richard Spender *Collected Poems*.

[4] *Listener*, August 23rd, 1945. Sidney Keyes and *Ha! Ha! among the trumpets*.

most conscious aspirants for a cheap and immediate notoriety.[1]

Critics want poets to write for their age rather than about their age, during the Second World War. They don't want to be presented with a problem as in the '30s, they want some kind of resolution and consolation. And although the younger writers are encouraged, with special mention for Keyes, Lewis, Fuller, and Comfort (Pudney, it is noted, speaks for quite a small group during the war – critics aren't always sure what to make of his easy exuberance), the writers who seem especially appreciated are Edith Sitwell, Richard Church, Day Lewis, Gascoyne, Spender, MacNeice – and there is even a call upon Auden, regretting his departure for America and suggesting that if he had stayed among the ruins of London he might have done what Aragon did for France in *Le Crève-Coeur*.[2] The nature of the war seemed to call for maturity and stature (which, it is complained, no poet really possesses).[3]

I have left until the end any mention of *Scrutiny*, because in many ways it either contradicts views discussed in this chapter, or it approaches them from a different angle. Also partly because it is a fairly easy periodical to run through and gather up one constant thread of opinion instead of a consensus, partly because it usually had the last word in any case by waiting until all other critics had expressed their views and then descending with its own criticism of those views, and partly because it issued this Manifesto when it first appeared in 1932 :

[1] *Spectator*, September 4th, 1942. S. Shannon reviewing Scarfe's *Auden and After*.

[2] *New Statesman*, July 11th, 1942. Raymond Mortimer reviewing Aragon's *Le Crève-Coeur*.

[3] *Spectator*, May 8th, 1942. S. Shannon.

> *Scrutiny*, then, will be seriously preoccupied with the movement of modern civilisation.[1]

In other words *Scrutiny* was aware of, and was going to comment on, the existing world situation as much as *New Country* or *New Writing*. Its awareness of the approaching war can be seen from its various articles on the subject. In 1932 for instance, G. Lowes Dickinson warned that war and capitalism were no longer 'academic' topics, they were now standing at the front door.[2]

It was determined, however, that it was going to criticise contemporary poetry not only as expressive of its day and age, but from the point of view of literature that lasts (not as many other critics approached it during the Second World War, as expressive of the human situation first and foremost). It therefore writes off a poet like Palmer as completely out of the range of fire if we take 'a serious interest in contemporary poetry'.[3]

It is of the 1930 poets that *Scrutiny* has most to say. In accordance with its dictates that poetry must, first and foremost be good literature before it can be praised for doing anything else, it cuts itself off from the merit awarded by other critics when they say that a poet like Day Lewis at least reflects his age. The reply of *Scrutiny* reviewing *A Time to Dance* is adamant:

> It is not poetry; it is Kipling-Newbolt. The Old Boy may have gone Left, but he remains true at heart to the Old School.[4]

The great criticism of the Auden–Spender school is

[1] May 1932, Vol. I, No. 1, 'A Manifesto'.
[2] May 1932, Vol. I, No. 1, 'The Political Background'.
[3] June 1934, Vol. III, No. 1. F. R. Leavis, 'Comments and Reviews'.
[4] September 1935, Vol. IV, No. 2. John Spiers on *A Time to Dance*.

levelled against their immaturity. Auden's talent is acknowledged, but like the 'poetical renaissance' which began with his 1930 *Poems* it has 'petered out in vapid mannerisms and stale clichés.'[1] Spender receives worse treatment; his *Trial of a Judge* is

> closet drama of the most barren kind. Mr. Spender has not had any greater success at coming to grips with life than he had in *Vienna*.[2]

What *Scrutiny* objects to is the inability of a poet like Spender to do what he says he is doing, or the worthlessness of what a poet like MacNeice succeeds in doing. Of *Autumn Journal* it remarks:

> in this present poem his feelings about such events as the September crisis do not, at their best, differ materially from those of the average sensible 'man in the street' and to his feelings about more personal topics the man in the street would be most often ashamed to own.[3]

But, adds *Scrutiny*, the book would not be worth reviewing 'did we not know that it will be acclaimed as a poem of 'some importance'. *Scrutiny*'s protest is frequently a guide to the way the wind is blowing.

On the whole we can sum up that protest as levelled against the unreality of the 1930 decade, the way the poets assumed positions for themselves, and the way in which they became outdated because their movement progressed no farther. It was a fairly common criticism about their productions by 1939:

> They are all identical and already have the quaintly lavendered air of a period-piece.[4]

---

[1] June 1940, Vol. IX, No. 1. R. G. Cox on *New Writing*.

[2] September 1938, Vol. VII, No. 2. W. H. A. Mason on *Trial of a Judge*.

[3, 4] June 1939, Vol. VIII, No. 1. W. H. Mellers on *Autumn Journal*.

Scrutiny, in fact, sees the 'pylon' poets as similar to the Georgians, an interlude in the mainstream of English literature, and adds that

> the prevailing tone of Cambridge's 'Poets of Tomorrow' (1940) has singular affinities with that of the day before yesterday.[1]

Perhaps in the end what we gather most clearly from *Scrutiny*'s criticism is the fact that the 1930 poets came sufficiently into the limelight and laid sufficient claim to a place of importance, for an attack to be levelled against them. Unlike Palmer, they cannot be completely out of the range of fire, for those who take 'a serious interest in contemporary poetry'.

[1] December 1940, Vol. IX, No. 3. W. H. Mellers on *Poets of Tomorrow: Cambridge Poetry of 1940*.